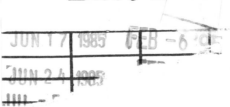

Tell Pa I'm Dead

◦O◦O◦

Also by Andy MacDonald
Bread and Molasses
Don't Slip on the Soap

Tell Pa I'm Dead

Andy MacDonald

1985

Doubleday Canada Limited, Toronto, Ontario
Doubleday & Company, Inc., Garden City, New York

Library of Congress Catalog Card Number 85-4382

First Edition

Design by Irene Carefoot

Typesetting by Compeer Typographic Services Limited

Printed and bound in Canada by D.W. Friesen & Sons Ltd.

Canadian Cataloguing in Publication Data

MacDonald, Andy
  Tell Pa I'm dead
ISBN 0-385-23142-3.
1. MacDonald, Andy. 2. Sidney Mines (N.S.) –
Biography. I. Title
FC2343.3.M33A36 1985   971.6′95′0924   C85-098319-3
F1039.C2M33 1985

I'm dedicating this book to my grandsons,
David and Michael,
who should be thankful they have me for a grandfather,
instead of Pa.

Contents

PART TWO

WE CAN'T BLAME PA FOR THIS

Preface

Well, if you don't know who I am by now, you should. I'm Andy. And my picture is on this book. At my age most people get homelier, but as you can see I'm getting prettier.

If you happen to run into me someday on the Trans Canada highway and you haven't read my first two books, *Bread and Molasses* and *Don't Slip on the Soap*, you won't be in conversation with me for more than three minutes before I'll tell you all about them.

Now in this, my third book, *Tell Pa I'm Dead*, there's the story about the day I was forced to go to school wearing a fish, the time Murray and I kidnapped a hydro pole, along with the day my twin and I decided to join Barnum and Bailey's circus with a crippled fly. There's also the day I took Teedy on an outing to paint the town red on just one package of needles; the time Murray hypnotized the school inspector; the sad day that I died, twice; and the morning I took Billy on his first visit to the dentist. Pa is just as strict in this book as in the last two, and we're still sent to bed at any time of the day.

Then all of a sudden in Part Two, I've grown up, believe it or not. In one story, you'll relive the horror Teedy and I went through at Pa's funeral when we had quite a scuffle with his ghost. Then there's the time Teedy and I were living in Virginia when we were accosted by a sadistic car salesman. You'll also find out how easy it was for me to quit smoking and how it would be for you too, if you like turnips. Then you'll marvel at the intricacies of my secret operation and be astounded about the night I went from being a pauper to a wealthy man and back to a pauper again, within a space of half an hour. You'll also be happy to read that our house is jinxed and that nothing ever works for us from the day we bring it home.

There are a lot more stories if you want to search for them. As for me, I'm not going to tell you any more. You can read them yourself. I'm too tired from writing this book. To heck with Pa, I'm going to bed on my own now.

So my advice to you is to put your feet in the oven, if the frying pan is out of the way, lean back in your chair, and get ready for a good laugh. It's always the best medicine for a sore head. And if you enjoy these stories, don't forget to drop me a line. I love hearing from readers and I'll answer you too.

Andy MacDonald
December 1984

Acknowledgments

I wish to thank:

Patrick Crean, my editor, who was and is a godsend, and the main reason my three books have been published; and who was amazed at the rubber tires that encircled the trunks of ninety-foot trees on my Dummy Farm.

Dianne Copp, my daughter, for straightening up and smoothing out crowded stories of mine to help make them more humorous.

Frankie, Dianne's husband, who even in the face of unexpected problems which popped up at this time, kept running around after tapes, papers, and ribbons for the typewriter. I know he lost weight.

Rhoda, my wife, who was thoughtful in that she typed my stories mainly in capitals, especially the nouns, making them much easier to read. And a special thanks to her for waiting on us hand and foot during our foul moods.

Pat Chambers, my nephew, for being so helpful in sharing his humour with us, although I want to steer clear of him on Lottery night.

My brother *Murray*, for funny reminders, and his old pyjamas.

My brother *Teedy*, for his hilarious letters, and his affection for me as his mother, when we were kids, including diapering.

My brother *Billy*, for his Dear John letters, and kisses.

My sister *Sophe*, for her generosity at the time I needed it most, giving me peace of mind to write.

My sister *Pearl*, for her swiftness in cleaning up the dishes, even after a supper of salt herring; and who thanked me so much for taking a chance and signing her bad report card while Pa was at a meeting.

My sister *Ann*, for her motherly affection to me, in nice letters.

My brother *Fred*, for his ready wit, and shots of VO and Schlitz.

My brother-in-law *Perce*, for showing me how to dye my hair and look young.

My sister-in-law *Ruth*, for having told all her friends in Ontario to buy my books.

My brother-in-law *Bob*, for encouraging me to quit smoking the first time in 1962. Maybe that's the reason I'm still here.

Rosemary and *Al Chiasson*; Rosemary for her love of my

kind of humor, which inspires me to write more, and Al for being Rosemary's guardian angel.

Carol and *Lester Roberts*; Carol for giving me a cup of tea any time I dropped in, and Lester for being the only man in the world who could fix our toilet (plumbers take note).

Tonie, *Eddy* and *Ross Goodwin*, my three foster children.

Even *Little Boy*, our seventy-year-old dog, a spayed female who, when the fire went out, lay on my feet and kept them warm while I wrote.

And a special thanks to my brother *Tennyson*, who passed away September 1984 in Halifax. He was one of my best promoters in the area, and we loved to trade shoes with each other. I can just see Tenny up there talking to Pa now, wearing a pair of my shoes. And I know what Pa will say when Tenny tells Pa about my first two books: "I hear it's got another book out called, *Tell Pa I'm Dead*. What will it think of next?"

Finally, thanks to Ma and Pa for having us, as without them you wouldn't know me or my brothers, or be reading this book for that matter.

PART ONE

◦○◦○◦

WE STAND ON GUARD
FOR PA

The Way We Were

∘C∘O∘O∘

This is probably going to sound like a broken record, after saying much the same thing at the beginning of my last two books, but here goes anyway.

Once upon a time, I was born into a family of thirteen, counting Ma and Pa, which included five girls and six boys. Another boy, David, died when he was about a year old. Our two older brothers and all of the girls, except for the baby, Pearl, had already left home when most of the incidents in this book happened to Billy, Murray, Teedy and me.

We were brought up during the depression years of the dirty thirties, and most of our friends and neighbours were as poor as we were. We often heard the story of one poor old man who couldn't pay his rent. Each time he had to clear the premises, about once a month, he had no means of conveyance to move the few things he owned – two chairs, a table, a bed and six banties – so he would call for a load of coal. And when the coal man came with it, the old fellow would say, "Don't dump it here," and then give him his new address. But first he'd get the coal man to pile up his furniture on top of the load of coal, plus his six banties, with their legs tied so they wouldn't fly off. It got to be such a common occurrence that as soon as the banties saw the coal truck coming in the lane, they would roll over onto their backs and hold their legs up in the air to have them tied.

We lived in Sydney Mines, a mining community on Cape Breton Island, in a big red square house built by Pa with his own nails. The house is still standing today, but it's now painted green. If Pa came back today, he'd probably burn it down. He hated green.

Eighty-foot cliffs that dropped off to the ocean below stood about a hundred yards from our house, and it was under those cliffs where I spent most of my days as a truant. During my few visits to school, I only learned one thing. This one thing I had to study for or be mangled by the teacher and picked apart by Pa. I stayed up half the night studying it, not knowing what it meant nor caring. I had it fully memorized. I still do. Believe me, it took me a lot more time to write it out for this book than it takes me to recite it. I can rope it out in fifteen seconds. If my old teacher could hear me spit it out today, she'd probably give me a job as an auctioneer. Anyway, here it is: "Proof that the earth is round: 1) when a vessel is coming in sight, a person on the shore first sees the top mast, then the lower mast, and lastly the hull. 2) A person travelling in the same direction can go around the world and come back to the same place from which he started. 3) If you look away to the horizon, the earth and sky seem to meet; the earth casts a round shadow." Amen. And all this time I'll bet you thought the earth was square.

Now, Pa worked in the mines, was a very strict parent, and a steady church goer. We always took our troubles to Ma, when she was alive, and she often saved us from certain punishment at Pa's hands. Until she died, when we four boys were in our early teens, she was our cushion from Pa's blasts and sentences.

Pa had lost two fingers in a mining accident and the stubs grew thick and boney. Many times when he wasn't sending us to bed in the middle of the day, or putting us in the cellar for some minor infraction, we would get a good clouting with those hardened stubs. So with this element of danger lurking in the background, we had to be resourceful, not only for our survival, but for our entertainment as well.

Our routine after Ma died was to get up at 4:00 a.m., get Pa's breakfast and make his lunch, and get him off to the mine by 5:00 a.m. He got home at 5:00 p.m., and it was between 5:00 a.m. and 5:00 p.m. that we took our rest. Saturday was guard day, when we walked in fear and trepidation around Pa. There was school through the week (when I went). And of course Sunday was the dullest day of all. Three times to church: once to Sunday School and twice to services with Pa. We detested this day of the week more than any other and would often wonder how much more of this boredom our minds could stand.

What we really hated during the sermon was the way the minister used his voice. He would start out very softly, then climb up the scale to almost a screech – then suddenly back down again to a whisper. Each week we'd be suffering through that long sermon waiting for the last blessed hymn, nearly asleep and just barely hanging in. The minister would begin something like this: "Be not deceived, evil communications corrupt good manners." His voice would be at its lowest and smoothest on the word "manners." We'd begin to get restless and itchy, thinking it was the end of the sermon. Even Teedy, the youngest, who slept through most of them, would look up as if he wasn't one bit sleepy. Then the minister would pause, for what seemed like five minutes. (We could have staked our lives that he was finished.) Then, *boom*, out he would come in a voice loud enough to rattle our inner ears: "A certain *man* from the land of *Egypt*. . . ." And on he'd go. That's when we'd really get upset and we'd glare at the minister as if to say, "Wasn't that the end? It should have been. Why in heavens name did you speak so low and then come to a complete halt. Do you know you're keeping us awake?"

We had no watches. Pa had one but he kept it in his pocket. I guess we could have interrupted the minister's dreaded sermon by saying "Hold it a minute!" and then asked Pa what time it was because we were sure the preacher had gone way over the scheduled hour. After ten more interminable minutes, during which we did our best to stop yawning and fidgeting, the preacher's story finally came to an end. We could tell for sure this time because the organist always returned to her seat. Thank God, we would think, and even Pa looked pleased.

After the boredom on Sunday, the four of us, Billy, Murray, Teedy and I, would often let off steam at night during the week while Pa was trying to get some sleep before 4:00 a.m. Our capers and whispering would often get to the stage of uncontrollable snickers. Then the voice of the Master would rock the still night. Pa would call the four of us to his bedside and after a few clouts on the rear or anywhere his fist landed, we would line up for sentencing. "Andy, you go in the dining room with the lights out; Murray, the kitchen, no lights; Teedy, the hall in the dark; and Billy, the front room." (The most fearsome place for man or beast to stay without lights.)

Pa was so strict, he made us get up from the supper table if we even sneezed. And we used to kid each other that we shouldn't be surprised if we went down to the cellar someday to find the kid next door had been put there three weeks before for something Pa didn't agree with. My twin, Murray, recalls an incident about a little girl who lived next door. She was about five and wanted to be an actress. So we would get her to practise on Pa. After he came home from work, we'd get her over and she would go into her act and say, "Cuna Moona, my Cuna Moona." Now no one knew what Cuna Moona meant, but it sure brought out the beast in Pa. Pa would say, "Get her away from me, she's foolish." Then she'd continue following Pa all over the place with her "My Cuna Moona" until Pa would say, "It will have to go home." (This was another habit of Pa's, calling anyone he was disgusted with, lost his patience with, or just plain couldn't stand, IT. Whenever he stopped using the person's name and jumped to IT, you knew he was making a big point.)

But this wouldn't stop the little actress. She'd keep right on going until he'd say, "Get out of here, you foolish flamer, or I'll put you where the neighbour's dogs won't bark at you." Then she'd go into her final act, saying to Pa, "Opie hand, Mr. MacDonald, opie hand." (By this she meant she wanted Pa to try to open her closed fist.) She would go on and on with her "Opie hand." Soon Pa was scuffling around the floor with her, trying to force her hand open. He'd get all worked up and say, "So help me God, you can't open *its* hand!"

Pa also had another habit. I don't know if he was having hot flashes or what, but he enjoyed going around barefoot; we were quite embarrassed by this. One time, walking this young girl to her home, I was shocked to see Pa's two-hundred-and-fifty-pound frame coming towards us down the street, bare-foot. The girl never knew what struck me as I almost broke her neck doing an about-face, so we wouldn't have to pass him. We kids always said it would be useless to have Pa play Santa Claus. He'd never fool us. We'd know it was him by his bare feet.

But no matter what else Pa was, he did have a great brain. He was president of the A.M.W. (mine worker's union) and also president of the Hospital Association for Nova Scotia. We all loved this about Pa because it took him away from Sydney Mines many times for his meetings.

During one of his meetings, we decided to have a wake.

Billy, a year older than me, was the slickest and fastest talker of the bunch. Somehow, he had got hold of a plaster of Paris pig's head. We worked all day making a casket for the pig out of two large wooden egg crates, nailed some black crepe over the front door and, as Pa was away at a convention in Halifax, we put his Masonic suit, his tall hat, and an extra pair of his glasses on the pig, and then laid the whole mess in the casket. We dimmed the lamps and took our places in the hall to receive condolences as was the custom.

We lived on a deserted street, kind of a lover's lane, so we had a few young people come over to review the remains of the dear departed. Shaking our hand, they'd say, "I'm sorry for your troubles." We were not too heartbroken, so Billy would reply, "Well, we've all got to go sometime." They would ask us who had passed on, and we'd say our father. So they'd go in to see him and pay their respects. They didn't know what to do then. They couldn't laugh right over the coffin because, for all they knew, that might have been the way Pa really looked after he died. (Maybe he'd had his face pushed in by a truck.) But as soon as they left the house, we could hear them going into hysterics.

One little fellow, who was quite a favourite of Pa's, came up to the house, with his eyes as big as saucers. On finding Pa had passed away, he commenced to cry. We took him into the room and he was so small, we had to lift him up to observe the remains. Still crying, he looked at the pig's head on Pa's clothes, shook his little head, tears dripping on the pig's face, and said, "Poor Pa, he used to give me a cent every Saturday when he got his pay." (By the way, everybody called Pa, Pa, even strangers. Even Teedy, when caught at some mischief one time and asked who his father was, answered: "Pa MacDonald.")

All of a sudden, we had an unexpected visitor. It was

Pa. He had come home early from his convention in Halifax. He tore into the house like Ferdinand the bull, put up the window shades, turned the lamps up bright, and beat us with the pig's head for having no respect for the dead. He gave me the worst going over, as he figured I was the instigator, and said, "I've a good mind to make use of the casket and put Andy in it." It was no good going after Billy. He'd have convinced Pa the pig jumped into the casket by itself.

Speaking of wakes, there was this time we attended a real wake for an old guy, nearly a hundred years old, and who had led a rugged life as a fisherman. All his life he'd rowed his dory against the tides in our area. As a result, he was all bent over with arthritis, in the same position as if he was rowing.

The undertaker had a heck of a time straightening him out. Finally, he laid him out on a piece of plywood and bound him up with strong black codline. At the wake things got pretty lively, and someone sneaked over to the casket with a knife and cut all the cords. The old fisherman sprung up in his casket, and one of the mourners went out, got a pair of oars, and put one in each of his hands, so that he appeared to be rowing his way to the cemetery – giving the impression that he didn't want to be a bother to those left behind.

Next came Murray, my twin, who was always hungry, and this one day he went to a meeting at the minister's house in Leitche's Creek. Wandering out into the pantry, he spied an apple and hoisted himself up onto the cover of a flour barrel to eat it. Immediately the cover flipped out from under him and he was jack-knifed into the half-full barrel. He couldn't get out and he was too ashamed to holler, but luckily the minister's wife found him there during supper, or he'd be there yet.

Murray was quite a prankster, and one time he got a Buck Rogers' badge out of a rolled oats box. He wore it a lot because it looked like a police badge. One night at a dance in Cranberry, he had the badge in his pocket. In those days, we all sat around the hall on benches and food was served along with the dance, for twenty-five cents. Each person would load up on refreshments (especially Murray) when the server, with plates of sandwiches and squares, passed by.

Murray spied a young girl reach out and take two or three helpings of everything that was pointed in her direction, sneaking half of it in her purse. He walked over to her, flashed his Buck Rogers' badge and grabbed her purse. He told her it was against the law to take more than her share, and she burst out crying, saying she was only taking some for her pet dog Benny's lunch in the morning.

Murray was also a very fast runner. He had to be. I guess that's why he was so slim – someone was always chasing him. Murray used to say he could run around in a circle so fast that no one could find him, because he'd be hiding in their vest pocket.

But one time Murray didn't fare so well in his running. He was hot-footing it home in a snowstorm, and he didn't see a neighbour's clothesline. Running as fast as he could, he got that sisal hemp rope right under the nose, and it threw him right back into the neighbour's yard. We were all sitting in the kitchen when he showed up at home, blood all over his face. He never said a word, just went straight to the knife drawer, grabbed the butcher knife and went back out again, with us all following along behind him wondering who he was going to murder, or whether he was just tired of living. He kept striding along until he came to the clothesline, and then he cut it to shreds!

Teedy, the youngest boy, was the most nervous and

highly strung of the lot of us. One night, when he was about ten, he was standing on this ledge looking in a window at a bunch of dancers. Grasping the window frame, he suddenly heard the voice of the Chief of Police roaring, "Get down from there this instant." Teedy ignored his command, not out of spite, but because of the shock of being cornered so suddenly like that. His plumbing started to leak and he couldn't find the shut-off valve for minutes.

Another time Teedy got into trouble was the day we were playing over at Priest's Field. It was about 11:00 a.m. and Pa was at home catching up on his sleep, as he had been on night shift the night before. Suddenly there was a big noise, and the first plane we had ever seen landed right before our eyes in the field!

This was too much for Teedy, so he took off for the house to wake up Pa to come see the airplane. He was almost hysterical, screeching and hollering and turning cart-wheels in front of Pa. Pa not only beat the stuffing out of Teedy for waking him up, but put him to bed where he couldn't even see the plane.

As for me, I well remember my first painting job. Murray and I had gotten this job to paint a neighbour's house red, ten shingles high, white, ten shingles high, and blue, ten shingles high. That's the way the man wanted it. I guess he was very patriotic. Anyway, it was a hot day and we were painting by the dining-room window, which was open. So I reached in and painted a dab of red on one side of the loaf of Co-operative bread that was sitting there. Little did I know that at tea time, we'd be invited in to eat the red bread.

Murray and I also used to follow the Salvation Army around when they were playing. There were these two young guys we knew who played horns in the Army. We'd get so disappointed when their jaws didn't burst like a frog when you put salt on it. Blowing their instruments, their cheeks would expand like balloons, but they'd never burst. One of the young guys would give us a sly look as if to say, "Ain't I good?" But we'd yell out: "Pa's right, he does have eyes just like a potato!" and run away as fast as we could.

Then there was the day I lost one of my nine lives, just like a cat. I had borrowed this guy's little red wagon. I got it going so fast down this steep hill, just pushing with my foot, that I didn't even know the wagon was out of control until I almost reached the bottom of the hill and found I couldn't get it turned. I hit the brick wall so hard that to this day I've still got a completely flat forehead.

Anyway, I think you've now got a pretty fair picture of how our family all got started once upon a time, thanks mainly to Pa. From here on, it's how we all lived happily ever after.

Someone Shot the Heel off My Shoe

◦○◦○◦

Nothing was more horrible to us than Sunday, the day we had to attend church three times: in the morning for the sermon, in the afternoon for Sunday School, and in the evening for still more preaching. We were Pa's little apostles. Why, with only a dozen or more sessions Teedy was about to leave home to get his papers to become a minister or even a nun. We spent so much time there that Billy once tried to walk on water, while I was ready to go and live with the Pope and Murray was fast becoming a deacon.

During these imprisonments, we had to dress with such care that we could have been presented before the Maharaji of Vendipore. This one Sunday I had gotten through the morning and afternoon sessions without mishap, but ran into big trouble just before the evening pilgrimage. We had just finished supper. Leaving nothing on our plates but the pattern, my brothers, Teedy, Murray, Billy and I single-filed upstairs to our clothes hangers, and very carefully slipped on our coats. If there had ever been a job available that required putting coats on hangers and taking them off, we would have gotten the job hands down. We spent more time doing this than hat-check girls. We looked each other over for sloppiness because we had to pass Pa's inspection each time before church.

Now, Pa was in the rocking chair in the kitchen, and there was no way we could get past him unless we went up the chimney in the front room. This time, I wished I had.

13

The heel had fallen off one of my shoes, and I could only walk as though half my leg was shot off. My brothers were standing in the hall planning a strategy for me so Pa wouldn't see my unheeled shoe. (I was praying that Pa would be struck blind, like Paul on the road to Damascus.) We discussed suggesting a quick game of blindman's bluff to Pa before church, but no one volunteered to bell the cat, or blindfold the Pa. Besides, asking Pa to play a game on Sunday would be like suggesting he kidnap the Minister. I even thought of telling Pa a vicious sniper lurking in the bushes had shot the heel off my shoe, but he would have asked to see the bullet hole.

It was my right shoe, and as I was to pass Pa on my right side, I thought I should just change shoes. But after considering this for awhile, I figured a left shoe on the right foot would be more conspicuous than a heel missing. Also my steering might foul up, and I might walk right into Pa's arms. If only I could have taken three steps with just my left foot, it would have taken Pa's eyes off my bad right one. While I might have been able to do that with skates on, I couldn't chance it. Skating on Sunday was punishable by death. We then considered the possibility of us all limping at once, but Pa would never have believed all four of us had sprained our ankles at the same time.

Murray figured if we chipped in all our old chewed-up gum, stuck to bed posts and under tables, and made one square lump, that it could pass as a heel – as long as I took most of the weight off that side. But Billy thought he had the best solution: a small wheel off the old organ stool was tied on the centre of my shoe, adding half an inch to one leg. Now I was all set to roll in to see Pa.

The door to the kitchen was opened and the parade started – Billy leading the way, then Murray, me and finally

Teedy. Billy was always in excellent sartorial shape and hardly merited a glance from Pa. I should have had Billy carry me out in his arms or push me in a baby carriage. He could have told Pa I was tired and wet; but I was a bit too old to be diapered. The trouble started when Billy cleared customs and opened the outside door to leave just as a neighbour walked in. Backing up to let the neighbour in, Billy immediately caused a walking jam. Then Teedy passed me from behind and left me in the most vulnerable position of all with my wheel spinning. The confusion of exits and entrances started a wobble on my crippled shoe and brought Pa's clear brown eyes to the tips of my toes, and back to my wheel. . . .

I was doomed. I was so close to Pa now I could see my reflection and a be-wheeled shoe in the pupils of his widening eyes. I noticed his body turning rigid, as though he was tensing before doing the sponge in yoga, or like a cobra would before it springs. (Rolling back and forth on my wobbly wheel I felt like doing a figure eight with Pa right around the room.) The other three soldiers had continued out the door, looking back toward the house and calling down the neighbour for getting in the way and messing me up.

Suddenly I was brought to attention by Pa, without a salute. But with the neighbour there, Pa's temper didn't reach a very high voltage. In his sweet voice, the praying one I accompanied many times in church, he told me to go to bed, implying to the neighbour that I was sick and should be in bed, instead of being in that stuffy old church.

What more could I expect? With Pa in the picture, ninety percent of our waking hours were spent in a prison bed. In a way I didn't mind because I could count my big penny collection and dream about what I'd splurge it on – if I was ever allowed out of bed again before they changed the coinage. In the meantime, while I was doing time in my room, Murray spied my missing heel outside the church, smuggled it home, and before Pa could figure out what had happened (he must have thought he had been hallucinating), we had it firmly stuck back on with some trusty well-chewed gum.

There's a Fish in My Pants

∘C∘O∘O∘

When sickness prevailed with someone in the family, every available cure was thought of at once by Ma and Pa. These amazing cures ran the gamut from eye of newt to hair of toad, from fish eyeballs soaked in molasses, goose grease for colds, to onion poultices, which would bring a boil to a head from across the room. We got a half teaspoon of kerosene for a sore throat, as long as you didn't smoke or blow out matches (if you did smoke, you wouldn't have to worry about your throat anyway, or even your life). Diarrhoea was cured by sitting on an empty bed pan for sixty-seven minutes with your eyes closed. And nagging headaches vanished with two hen feathers scorched to a dull brown inserted in each ear.

Although there weren't any favourites in our family of twelve kids, when one of us was sick, he or she became the immediate centre of attention, in case it was the last we saw of our sickly sibling. And you had to get better even if they killed you in the attempt. If the proper procedure wasn't pursued, a sore throat and headache were considered fatal. And without the right cure for scarlet fever, dyptheria, or spinal meningitis, you wouldn't even get reincarnated.

One cold winter's night, I awoke to discover I was in the process of dying. No one could have been as sick as I was and still remain alive. My tongue was too large for my mouth and dry, like I had a big woollen mitten for a tongue. My head was aching on all four sides and I had to prop it up with my hands, and try not to breathe.

17

My three brothers, asleep in the same bed, were in their glory. Wracked with fever, I was keeping them blissfully warm. I inched my way toward the edge of the bed and fell into a chair in the darkness. The room was in the zero range, the windows coated with frost. Shuffling and groaning started up in the bed as my brothers tried to warm up after having lost their heating pad.

Thumping along the floor with my feet like hot-water bottles, a sister woke up and came running to our room. In minutes I was wrapped in swaddling blankets and led downstairs to an unoccupied couch. Then ten drops of nitre were administered to my corpse. I soon felt as though all my skin was dropping off me like ice off a tin roof. The fever slowly vanished and, like Sleeping Beauty when she was kissed by the Prince, I could feel my limbs easing back to life.

Next morning when Pa learned of my sickness, I admitted to him that I now only had a slight sore throat. That nevertheless brought on one of Pa's cures, handed down from a long line of sea captains. It couldn't be refused under any circumstances. A salt herring, which was supposed to draw the poison from my throat, was tied on a string and hung around my neck like the Ancient Mariner's albatross.

How could I appear in school with a fish caressing my thorax? It was bad enough to have the smell of salt herring on my breath from supper the night before. But I wouldn't be here today if I'd have defied Pa. So the herring was tied with a slipknot over its scaley neck and hung upside down about an inch below the hollow of my throat, doing a nose dive into my pants. Then off fishy and I went to school, just like Mary and her little lamb.

Never being too bright in class, it always seemed fate was waiting to torment me. And this fish-filled day, the teacher called on me and my little fish to go to the map and show the class the different countries we were studying. Why me? There were fifty other kids there and I'll bet not one sported a herring necktie. I should have pointed to the Atlantic and told them, "And this body of water is the abode of the creature that is hanging around my neck."

A high turtle-neck sweater hid the herring from view, but I looked like a child with a good sized goitre forming in his collarbone; either that or a misplaced breast. Why couldn't the teacher have asked me instead, "Andy, would you please describe a fish, and tell us where they are found." I'd have had the answer to that: "They are scaley, salty, stinky, and they are found around my neck."

I did manage to find a couple of countries on that map, but still searching and mumbling with pointer in hand, the class became curious as to what I was doing. Sweating with excitement and nerves, and fidgeting as if a bra strap had broken, I kept making frantic clutches at my throat. I probably looked like I was trying to strangle myself – obviously a case of dual personality. But my pores were absorbing the salt from the herring and causing a terrific itch. Twisting almost in half for relief, the worst happened. The herring string broke. I now tried my best to hold the herring in my pants. How could I face my friends if a herring fell out on the floor? A live one, not so bad: I could tell them that I fell in the ocean on my way to school. But a twisted salt herring with a string tied to it? My Lord, my girlfriends would think I kept a salt herring in my pants as a pet on a leash.

The itchy herring slid slowly but relentlessly down over the full length of my body and lodged in the tight cuff of my long johns. To anyone in the vicinity watching me closely, it looked like I was flexing my muscles like a body builder, first my chest, then my stomach, thigh muscles, then my leg; either that or parts of my body were dropping off into my boots.

I was at the point of coming straight to attention in front of the class and saying, "Okay, this is it. The jig's up. I have a dead fish in my pants. So what are you all going to do about it? If you have any complaints, talk to Pa." Then I would have bent down, ripped the mushy fish from my pantleg and flung it down the teacher's neck since it was her fault that I was up there in the first place.

The teacher finally told me to take my seat, knowing she wasn't going to get any more information out of me. Why, the fish knew more about geography than I did. As I walked back, the fish's tail suddenly slid out from the cuff of my long johns. But no one noticed it or felt it but me. I knew as long as I took tiny baby steps, the rest of the fish wouldn't appear. With titters all round the class, I crept back to my desk like a turtle. I was sorry I hadn't put a fishhook and line in the herring's mouth, then I'd have had control of my fish and could have reeled it in.

Finally the bell ran, and I turtle-shuffled it right out of school and out of sight of the rest of the kids. With no one around to see, I ripped the heathen creature, which now resembled an old rolled up leather mitt, out of my cuff, grasped it in my hand, and with a raspy sore throat intoned, "From water you cameth, to water you goeth," as I flung old fishface over the cliff. I just hoped that Pa wouldn't ask for the herring back so we could have it for supper.

That evening Pa swelled with pride when I told him his herring had cured my sore throat (not to mention my breathing). Little did Pa know that I now had a stomach ache. I didn't dare tell him for fear he might have presented me with a tuna to take to school. At least it wouldn't have fallen out the leg of my pants. But I'd probably have had to straddle it and ride it to school, and then cradle it against my stomach all day when I got there.

After this fishy episode, sore throats came again over the years, but I never complained of them to Pa, even if my voice sounded like the Big Bad Wolf's. The only way I was going to try that cure again was in the jungle, alone, sporting a fig leaf.

The Broken Teapot

∘C∘C∘C∘

I couldn't count the times I heard Pa tell visitors who came to the house that his teapot, given to him by his long dead mother, had been handed down through generation after generation. We even heard that it was once used by the King of England as a paperweight.

There's such a thing as being too careful, as I was when I knocked it off the stove one day and it broke into ninety-one pieces, a piece for each year it had reigned. About twelve then, I immediately stopped growing and aged considerably, as did my brothers. In my mind I could see the old King wandering aimlessly searching for his paperweight and then gesturing for me to come sit on his papers as a replacement for the teapot.

Luckily Pa was at a union meeting when I annihilated his pet teapot. So an urgent meeting was held among the four of us to find out what we should do. We wondered if we should have a seance to summon up our dead grandmother and tell her to get us another teapot. Billy suggested that we tell Pa the King's ghost had come back to retrieve his prized teapot paperweight, that he couldn't rest in peace until he had it. Then, we wondered if we could get someone to kidnap Pa after his union meeting and keep him until we grew up. Or maybe we could disguise the house so that Pa would walk right by it without ever recognizing it.

We couldn't even write an angry letter to the teapot company to tell them their teapot had leaped off the stove and thrown itself onto the floor because the Royal Family would then find out we had their teapot, and would probably declare war on us. Visions of the Tower of London raced through our minds.

With no money to buy a teapot that resembled Pa's in any way, we had to make do with the porridge dish to make tea for Pa and the rest of us, without letting Pa know his teapot had bitten the dust. As Ma was away visiting our relatives in Boston during this time, we took turns getting Pa off to work in the mine at 4:30 a.m. each day. This alone made our lives worth living. Preparing his breakfast gruel, we would quickly switch his porridge to a bowl, rinse out the porridge dish, then make the tea in it. We had a ten-gallon soup pot besides the lone dipper for porridge. But we knew Pa would ask questions if he saw us make porridge in that pot. Like magicians, if Pa came too close, we'd switch the dipper around out of sight. We got adept at it every day. With lots of conniving and sleight-of-hand tricks, we did wonderfully for the first week. Until Friday evening. Everyone was happy, because Pa was getting ready to be off to another meeting. (Pa and meetings were made for each other. If he wasn't at a union meeting, he'd be at a church meeting or a Mason meeting.)

A sharp rap came at the door. There stood two Indians. She was holding baskets and he had clothes props to sell. Supper dishes were on the table and on our stove the little porridge dish peeked out from behind the big soup pot, then appeared to back in again. Indians had the same outlook on food as we did. We were all paddling the same canoe. If a neighbour had given them a lunch a half hour before, and we then asked them to eat with us, they'd never refuse even if they had to stuff it in a basket, their pant pockets or under their hats. And neither would we.

Pa always asked people to stay and have a cup of tea,

bless his heart, and this day was no exception. Then, as if we had been trained by cooks in the Navy, the four of us dashed for the porridge dish, which contained a spoonful of water and a ball of used tea leaves.

The woman kept talking about Indian tea. Then she got up and strolled toward the stove. I knew we should have tied her up to her baskets and thrown her over the cliff. As she came toward us, Billy lunged in front of her like an octopus defending its young. Perplexed, she decided to return to her chair in case we decided to tackle her from behind and scalp her.

Everything was going quite well until the woman asked a fatal question while Pa was waiting for his refreshing pick-me-up. We brew our tea in clay pots. It makes the tea taste better. How come you don't have one?" Why couldn't they and paleface Pa have gone down fighting like Custer at the Battle of the Little Big Horn?

Pa quickly scanned the stove for his mummy's teapot. Scrambling desperately, we prayed for Teedy to faint from fright, just to get the heat off us. "What in Heaven's name happened to the old teapot?" he said in a low voice. We had visitors, so Pa didn't use his tall voice; he just threw a knowing and killing smile at us. He looked at Teedy, the youngest, first. Without a blink, Teedy said, "It melted." That would have been all right, if it had been made of bubble gum, but there had not been any bubble gum during the reign of the old King. We wished Pa could have melted.

Just as he was about to send us to the guillotine, the car taking Pa to the union meeting pulled up in our driveway. We were saved by the union bell. Pa left, mumbling in Hebrew, and we were left alone with the company. They were now at our mercy, and we almost pushed them out the door. Billy, the game one, was even thinking of jamming one of the woman's baskets over the Indian's head and heaving him out, while shooting arrows at her.

After a few days, when Pa had come out of his coma brought on by the loss of his mother's antique teapot, he bought a new one. We had convinced him that we had seen little pieces fall off the old teapot on numerous occasions, but figured it was just soot. We then told him that one day it had just disintegrated before our eyes like a big marsh-mallow. Pa had a tear in one eye as he related how his mother had gotten it from her grandmother, while he was just a gleam in our grandfather's eyes. Amazed at his calm mood, we thought he was sick – and wished he was. But we thanked the Lord and managed to put on a sad face as Pa looked us over in the half-lit kitchen. He then spoke up and said, "You know, I should have been in bed long ago." We heartily agreed. And as Pa's sad footsteps disappeared, Teedy, Murray, Billy, and I, tapped the table lightly with a spoon, and said, "Case dismissed." Then we regained our lost weight, our youth and our sanity (now that Pa had lost his) while we made ourselves a good fresh cup of tea in the new tea-pot, without pieces of porridge or arrowheads floating around in it.

Yo Ho Heave Ho

◦◦◦◦◦

The long cold winters on Cape Breton Island usually started in October and continued until June. So with nearly nine months of cold, we had to be able to start the coal stove every morning with good kindling wood. Pa had us four boys trained in late summer to get as much waste, boards, driftwood or anything containing wood from along the many miles of shoreline. I believe we even burned parts of the *Titanic*, as it sank not far from us. Pa wasn't the type to tell us to keep anything for sentimental reasons. Into the stove it all went.

Every inch of our woodshed was piled high with rows of wood all cut the same length to fit the stove. Our other old shed was now shaped like a tired old man, bent over, hands resting on his knees, as if to say, "I can't stand no more." This other shed protected our many tons of coal from the rain and the snow. You could always see one of us on the way home from school, dragging an old board or a few blown-off shingles, like a beaver on the way to his dam.

Early one winter, it rained for two days. Then with a sudden drop in temperature, the rain froze as fast as it fell. With this silver freeze-up, wires, trees and hydro poles built up so much ice that the weight snapped them like blades of grass under a lawn mower. The next day hydro wires and poles were down for miles, hundreds of them, and there was no power for weeks.

Murray and I took advantage of the situation when we

overheard a conversation in the post office that those hydro poles made the best cedar kindling a man or a woman could burn. My eyes met Murray's. We were going to get one if we had to get Paul Bunyan and Babe, the blue ox, to pull it for us. Of course, we'd have to hide it from Pa because he would have said, "Take it back and put it exactly where you got it, or I'll have you both arrested." He would have told us, like Pilate, that we had stolen from Caesar, and now we'd have to carry our cross to our grave, after which he'd have hoisted the pole onto our sad, tired shoulders.

But we were going to take our chances. Our trail started a cold blustery Saturday in December. We decided to try to polenap a hydro pole, one as close to home as possible, and then get it to a spot behind the house where Pa wouldn't be looking out the window (he might have rolled the pole back over us with one boot, tied us to the stake and lit a match).

Skulking through the gloomy late afternoon, we soon came upon one. There she lay, quiet and still, a full-grown hydro pole. Motionless, we gazed upon it and tried to imagine all the kindling wood we would recover from the carcass. We soon found out that a hydro pole is quite heavy for two boys who together weighed a hundred and ninety pounds, but we were going to get this one even if, like the mountain to Mohammed, we had to move our house to where it had fallen. This would have been easier if our town had only had fifty-foot-wide ditches. Then we could have rolled the poles into the water, stood on them, and told anyone who inquired that we were in a log-rolling contest, while we hot-footed on our wooden treadmill right to our doorstep.

As it was, the way we manoeuvered that pole was something to see. At one point, we were in a field running parallel with the road. Traffic was passing by quite steadily. Now we didn't want anyone to see us, so we lay down on our backs, with me on one end of the pole and Murray on the other, and began pushing and rolling the pole with our feet. That way the people on the road couldn't see us moving the pole. In the growing darkness, Murray said, "Let's make this more interesting," and then told me what he was thinking: searching for this hydro pole was like hunting for fuel for the family. The wood would bring heat and warmth for all to enjoy. Why, we were just like Robin Hood and Little John on a foray into Sherwood Forest, searching for firewood to bring back to our Merry Men. Sure, you weren't supposed to take hydro poles. There was lurking danger from the Sheriff of Nottingham and Pa, but Robin and Little John had experienced danger too. Inspired by this noble example from history, we were off again.

We had just rolled over two frozen dead cats when Murray remarked that he didn't think Robin and Little John would have gone to this extent to get supplies. "For the Merry Men, Murray," I said, "it's for the Merry Men." With that, a look of pride and determination appeared on Murray's face and we began to push again. For about an hour, Murray repeated "heave ho now," like a Volga boatman. Inch by inch, caterpillar fashion, wriggling across the ice-covered field, we advanced very slowly.

Suddenly, Murray hollered "heave ho" as loud as he could, which caught me off guard as we were supposed to keep our voices low. I jumped up, ran to him, and whispered, "What happened?" He had rolled right through a plop of half-frozen cow manure and it was all over his back. He shouldn't have been too upset though because he was able to slide better now, and anyway the smell wasn't too ripe what with the frost. We wondered what Robin Hood and Little John would have done in a situation like this.

Then we had to figure out how to get a fifty-foot pole under a barbed-wire fence with posts twelve feet apart. If this had been a legal pole, we could have asked Pa to put on a pair of kilts and toss the caber (hydro pole) over the fence, like they do in Scotland. Somehow, we snaked that pole through the fence sideways. Now to make matters worse, in the centre of this pole was a large spike screwed on in the shape of a hook. We had tried our best to screw it out by hand, but to no avail. It was bothersome because when we were rolling the pole, the spike would act as a brake against our pumping efforts. We also had to be careful not to get stabbed to death by it. So, after an hour of pushing, grabbing and lifting, we were only ninety feet along, and our backs were crooked with strain. But we knew that no matter what, we would get this pole to our yard; hopefully before we were eligible for our old age pensions.

Finally, we stopped and sat on the pole, as though we were viewing the harbour at night. Against the street lights we could see a heavy-set man coming our way. He was a fisherman we knew, taking a short-cut home. It was okay to tell him our story, as we knew he wouldn't tell Pa or the hydro people. We confided in him so much that we offered him a job. He would be our Friar Tuck.

"You push from the centre," Murray told him, as the man tried without success to unscrew the long spike. But during the first roll over, the hook attacked his heavy coat and sheered the cloth in a circular manner, just like peeling an apple with a paring knife. We halted our push and offered our deepest sympathy. His coat was torn down the side and there were small rips in his pants. Poor Mr. Tuck. But after this mishap, the Friar sort of went mad, saying, "We'll get her there some way." Instead of stopping and going home, he became furious and more determined than ever to deliver that pole. It looked to Robin and I that Friar Tuck wanted this kindling wood more than we did. We prayed he wouldn't take it from us later, before we had a chance to show it to our band of Merry Men. All in position again, with our Friar off-centre now, away we went. Advancing with more speed, we had strong help. The Merry Men would salute our gallant efforts. We would be heroes in our time.

All at once, a sudden push combined with the slippery cow plop wound Murray around the pole like a snake on a limb. As we slid him out from under, he cried as he showed me two buttons and a pocket that had been ripped off his school coat. After this close call, much of the time was spent with Murray watching me and me watching Murray to make sure our clothes wouldn't get caught anymore. More and more our Friar was pushing the pole all by himself, with the strength of an ox. And it seemed the more Friar Tuck tussled and shoved, the crazier he got. So we kept a close watch on him, too, along with our clothes. When we were nearly home, and he looked as though he'd been torn by a savage bear, he said, "Well, boys, you don't have far to go now." Thanking him, we waved goodbye to our crazy old fisherman Friar, who was now walking down the lane, mumbling to himself in Swahili, with his shredded coat flapping in the crisp December wind.

Rolling the pole into our yard in triumph, we swivelled it around to fit into the garden so it wouldn't be under the fence in the neighbour's yard. We then covered it with dirt like a cat covering its litter to hide all traces. Back in the house, and trying to settle in quietly with our other brothers (the Merry Men), we whispered and said, "We have enough kindling until the year 2000." Then we told them about our hidden haul. Everything was mum.

Pa read the evening paper daily, and when he'd forget it on his way home from work, he'd send one of us to town for it. Billy was picked this evening to get it. Upon his return and before giving the paper to Pa, he sneaked around the house and called to Murray and I, saying, "Look at the headlines," as he read mournfully, "Enterprising thieves steal hydro poles." Murray's freckles stood out a deep brown against his ashen face, as we thought Friar Tuck must have squealed on us already. Billy read further on about how the police were on the trail, and the heavy jail terms we were in for. We went into a state of shock.

One thing was for certain: Pa must never know. For if he did, Robin and Little John's efforts would go unheralded. There would be no flags and banners, no box of medals, no proud salutes – only the sound of Pa's hammer erecting a scaffold for our execution. And Pa would probably use lumber from the outhouse to build our gallows. In a carefully thought out plan, we could visualize him removing only certain boards, so that when any of our surviving brothers occupied the outhouse, they would feel the cold wind blowing through. Shaking and shivering, they would remember why Pa had removed the boards and immediately think of Murray and me and the crime we committed. The image of us swinging in the breeze would deter them from any similar felony.

Realizing we hadn't dug a deep enough trench for our wooden pole corpse, and with darkness descending over the earth, we put on our coats, shoes and heavy socks (our mittens), and with a half shovel and a toothless fork, we started to bulldoze a deeper grave like ghoulish body-snatchers. We had lots of inside help. Billy and Teedy were covering for us in the house. Now if Pa were to be taken suddenly by the call of nature, he'd pass close by us on the way to the outhouse. If he did, we were to freeze like grave markers and blend in with the pole in the dark. In case this happened, Billy had a white sponge ball that he'd throw from an upstairs window. If we saw a bouncing rubber ball, we knew it meant, "Beware, the Sheriff is close by."

Murray and I frantically continued our spading, feeling like gophers digging for their lives before something ate us. After nearly two hours of prodding and heaving mud, our mammoth toothpick was finally covered up level with the ground. Feeling as though we were financially set for life, Murray and I retired to the house in a deep state of relaxation for a change. No one could find that pole now, even if they brought in archaeologists. And when a six-inch layer of snow covered the land, we hardly knew the spot ourselves.

For one week, the papers blasted the thieves. Then we found out what the newspapers were talking about. Big two-ton trucks had been taking away entire poles, and the copper wire along with them. So it wasn't Robin Hood and Little John they wanted, after all.

A few night later, Pa looked at Billy and said, "Do you think you fellows could bring home a broken pole or two. I was talking to the hydro manager, and he said they would be only too glad to get them out of the road." It was the first warm smile I got from Murray for days when I caught his wink, as he flicked it to me from behind Pa's left ear.

Next morning, after much poking, digging and prying, we brought our pole back to the surface. When Pa arrived at 5:00 p.m., we smothered a happy laugh, as we rolled along on our pole like squirrels on a treadmill. After orders from Brigadier Pa, we spun that huge kindling around like a cigar. Our final trick was for Robin and his Merry Men to cut our pole up into stove-length pieces to warm the porridge of the Sheriff of Nottingham, alias Pa.

The Day We Salvaged a Cow

◦○◦○◦

Living with the ocean all around us, we were always waiting and watching for a rowboat to leave a schooner and
drift wildly in to shore just beneath the cliff our house was
on. That would mean the boat was ours, if we were fast
enough to scramble down and get it before someone else
did and tie it to our bedstead. Salvaging was the law of the
sea, kind of like finders keepers, losers weepers.

One day, Billy and I were coming home from town
when, to our surprise, we came across a huge Guernsey
cow on the loose. She was in the middle of the road, with a
hundred-foot rope tied round her neck, and we knew she
wasn't a rowboat. Rowboats didn't have horns. But we were
going to salvage this cow if we had to pasture it in Pa's
bedroom (after first disposing of Pa's body). Holding the rope
very tightly, we weren't going to ever let her go. If our cow
had decided to jump over the moon, Billy and I would have
gone flying right through the air along with her and the cat
and the fiddle.

Now, we figured we knew the owner of the cow. She
lived about three miles from the salvage spot. We used to
buy a pint of milk now and then from her, when we ran out.
But we were sticking to the finders keepers law of salvage.
The cow was now ours, lock, stock, and udder.

We fed the huge beast grabs of grass until dark. Then
we led her toward home. Just out of sight, Billy stayed with
the cow, pulling grass, while I ran on ahead to see where Pa

was situated in the house. Through the window, I could see him seated as usual in his favourite rocker, reading about the price of beef. It would have been pretty hard to talk Pa into thinking Mrs. Moo was a dory that had washed ashore, so our big worry now was how to keep the cow from mooing. Every ten steps she took, she let out with a terrific moo, as if to say, "Man oh man, I'm tired and lost. Take me home. I don't like what you fellows are up to. You're complete strangers to me."

It's not easy to keep a cow from mooing, unless it's hanging by its tendons from an S hook. We tried though. Slipping our hands over her big, slippery open mouth, we nearly wrestled her to the ground, but only ended up with slobbers and hard stares from the cow. With a shorter rope we tethered bossy behind an old woodshed. Then we noticed someone looking out a neighbouring window as we were putting our cow behind the building. It was getting quite dark now, so Billy whipped off his long black coat, and we each held a part of it in front of the cow. Whoever was watching left the window, figuring it was just something on our clothesline. The cow now only got out a muffled moo once in a while, because by this time we had made a muzzle for her from Billy's belt.

Two days and a night went by without Pa knowing we were raising cattle. Our problem now was the udder. It was loaded with milk and nearly as big as the cow. On the first night we looked out the window and Billy said, "I believe there's a calf out there, laying beside the cow." On closer inspection in the moonlight, we found the calf was the cow's udder. She was so big, we didn't dare go near her with anything sharp. Ice picks, knitting needles, scissors, barbed wire, or porcupine quills were banned from the area. When she took a side-ways turn, milk would squirt from her teats like rain from a leaky roof.

What could we do? We couldn't milk her. No one had

ever showed us how. We might have given it a try, but we were scared to death we'd pull off her udder. It seemed obscene in a way, anyway, and we knew Pa wouldn't have wanted us touching her private parts. But we did take good care of her. She was well-fed, well-brushed, and well-talked to, as we studied every muscle and hair follicle. But we knew that we were in a danger zone and that any day now her bag would burst – possibly drowning a third of the population of Sydney Mines in milk. What a way to go.

The second night, after doing nothing all day but watch Pa's comings and goings through a knot hole in the barn and pulling grass for the hidden cow, we washed our green hands that now looked like they belonged to the Jolly Green Giant and then retired for the night, or so we thought.

It was a noiseless summer's night, beautiful, calm, and warm. Pa opened his window much higher than usual to coax in a breeze. At 11:00 p.m., either the cow took a lonesome spell, or was going into milk spasms, because she started mooing in triplicate. The belt must have slipped off her rubbery snout. I told Billy I thought it was Pa sighing, but the second sigh was definitely a loud urgent moo. I looked at Billy and said, "It's the cow." If we hadn't had so many stairs to climb with her, and if we didn't have to pass Pa's bedroom, we would have taken her to bed with us, even if one of us had to sleep on the floor. The lonesome moos wore on. If Pa had liked western music, jazz, opera, or even the blues, I could have sung loudly accompanied by Billy to cover the moos, but Pa hated those kinds of music.

Pa's room was two doors from ours on the opposite side of the cow, so Billy and I took turns coughing each time the cow mooed. After more than ten minutes of hacking and choking, and hoping Pa had fallen into a sound sleep, we ran out of coughs. But the cow was still full of moos. Pa gave a sleepy yell from his room, "I hear a cow –

must be on a ship passing by." Billy had the audacity to tell Pa he didn't hear a thing, thinking Pa would now go to sleep and dream he was herding a drove of cattle across the ocean.

An hour later, she was still mooing, and Pa hollered in, "That beast must have swum to shore. Can't you fellows hear it? You must be deaf!" Billy and I huddled in whispered consultation. We told Pa we'd go out and look around. With no flashlight, no moon, and no sleep, we took a few matches with us. Stumbling our way to the back of the shed, we spied our inflated cow lying down. The weight of her udder must have capsized her. And she was so wrapped up in the rope that she only had about one inch of it left to move about on. It was the equivalent of being hung. She couldn't get up and our homemade muzzle had worked its way off and was down underneath her so she had plenty of mouth to wake up Pa with her death-rattle moo.

Lassoing her by the light of a match, Billy fit the rope back around her neck and we both pulled on the rope until she got to her feet. We then took the shortest route we could back to the woman who owned the cow. We'd had more than enough hassle and besides we were getting tired of our secret cattle rustling.

A half hour later, we were wondering what to say to Mrs. MacLarren about her cow-napped bovine. We decided to tell her that we had just found her mooing out by our outhouse. We also told her that by the looks of the cow she should milk her that very second before we were all washed away in a flood of milk.

After this close call, we just kept our eyes on the ocean, looking for dories and such, or possibly a runaway train. At least we wouldn't have had to feed it. And the next time we saw a lost cow, we treated it with the same respect as the sacred cows in India.

The Time We Moved to Boston

❀❀❀

One of our older sisters, Helen, was going to Boston to live with another older sister, Grace. Helen soon had her train ticket, and after her dilapidated suitcase was packed, we walked her to the station, two miles away. All the way home we wished we were Helen going to Boston, the only city we had heard of since we were able to listen. We figured she'd probably live there for the rest of her life, on the train.

In a month's time our daily routine was pepped up because we got a letter from Helen, saying she'd gotten a job in a gum factory. (We weren't allowed to speak to Pa with a full chaw, but we chewed gum on the side.) A gum factory! We were addicted to gum. We'd almost rather have chewed gum than eat supper. How lucky could you get, I thought, as I threw away my six-week-old blob of gum. About the only thing better would have been a job in a jaw-breaker factory.

Helen said she liked her job. Who wouldn't, in a gum factory? But by the end of the letter, you could tell she was getting lonesome. To hide her sorrow, she ended with a "P.S. Tell the kids I'll send them some gum." This was something we'd never forget. Gum from the States, and our sister making it with her own two hands! We told everyone in town, and wondered if there was some way to get the news into the Speech from the Throne.

Our anticipation was great. For days we looked in candy store windows. We told our friends that the gum our sister was sending us would be ten times better than the stuff they were chewing. We came close to raising Helen to sainthood, finally coming to believe that she'd actually invented gum. Teedy would hold a mirror up for us while we practised our jaw movements, getting in shape for our gum chewing.

What a glorious feeling it was the day we went to the post office and they told us there was a parcel for us. We almost crawled through the small wicket to get it. We even loved our enemies then, the ones who hung out in the old post office to get warm. Smiling constantly the whole mile home, our jaws were getting ready.

At home the door to the kitchen was held open for us while we entered like visiting dignitaries – bowing like the Chinese. Tired faces lit up as we tossed the awkward bundle on the table, saying, "Get the scissors!" Ma snipped the string close to the knot (to save it for fishing lines) and opened the treasure we were waiting for. She unfolded different pieces of clothing with small notes attached to each saying "hope they fit." In a small brown paper bag were fifty sticks of gum, the most we'd ever seen at one time. We didn't eat supper that evening. Instead we had a kind of ceremony in which we chewed gum for hours, just like cows chewing a continuous cud. And not just one piece of gum, but ten sticks at once as our mouths laboured away trying to take care of them all. I'd have been proud to have had the mouth of a moose.

Pa wasn't home from work yet, so we walked outside into the yard to tell our friend, Stooky, about the parcel, and to let him watch us chew. Trying to make him as happy as we were, we soon gave him one stick of gum.

Pa then arrived from the mine and Murray, back in the house, overheard a conversation he was having with Ma about selling the house and taking the whole family to live in Boston. Murray brought the news outside to us. We hardly knew our names, we were so happy, and could have flown to Boston right then without a plane. We kept telling Stooky we'd send him parcels. He was almost as excited as we were, drinking in the dream world of gifts, new jobs, and endless supplies of juicy gum. We told him there would be lots of food, big cars, rich people, ice cream, theatres, zoos, circuses, big buildings, pretty girls, pie, pop, no school, no church, new shoes, the odd cigarette, chocolates, radios and plenty of gum.

Murray rushed back inside the house for added hysteria about Pa's fast decision – the trip to Never Never Land. Before too long Murray was out to us again, saying, "Pa's talking about suitcases!" I don't know why he was talking about suitcases, as we four brothers could have carried all our belongings in our back pocket, travelled light, and floated down south in a blimp.

Feeling like the Vanderbilts about this time, the four of us came to an agreement. We would donate our chaws of gum (that had been chewed to death) to Stooky. As if hypnotized, Stooky added our huge wads to his lone stick. Although he had no room for his voice to seep through to thank us, we helped him by shoving in the last stick, as Murray finally forfeited his blob. Stooky now was chockfull of chaws. His jaws would no longer function. The boy had forty-one sticks of gum in his mouth, and was still standing.

But we still expected him to answer us and we asked him if he'd like to come away with us. Stooky could hardly breathe, he could barely nod his heavy head. All he could do was throw his arms around like a sick penguin who needed a doctor. With lots more room in our mouths, we could now share our excitment with each other over the things we were going to get – scooters, Indian suits, a pair of rubber boots. All these things seemed free where Pa was to make this big move in life. Why, we might even take a trip to Washington and live with President Hoover for awhile, if he didn't mind. And why would he mind? We'd be bringing him gum.

Leaving Stooky propped up on an old bench, Murray ran back happily to the house, almost out of his mind, and at the point of telling Pa that he'd always loved him and not to forget the pot under the bed.

We were still sitting, smiling, and waiting for answers from Stooky's full mouth, watching him slowly turn blue from lack of breath, when Murray arrived back on the scene. We sensed a revolutionary change in the atmosphere. In the past minutes Murray had aged, acquired a limp, and gone completely white. He said he had asked Ma when we were leaving for Boston and she had said, "We aren't going, dear, it would cost a fortune to move there, and besides you children are settled in school." If it had been me they were worried about pulling out of school, they needn't have worried. I had been on one hundred and forty-two years of truancy, including several past lives, and I'd loved every minute of it.

Ma had said Pa couldn't leave the mine or we'd starve. (We wouldn't even have minded starving.) We wished Murray had gone into the wrong house to get the bad news. We were so mad at him we could have sealed him in a tomb of well-chewed gum.

Hearing sad moaning noises, our eyes now wandered to Stooky's lumpy jaws. His jaw had now jammed shut and Teedy muttered, "Can we have our gum back?" Slowly, prying his mouth open, Stooky forfeited the forty-one chaws, one by one, inhaled his first good deep breath in over an hour, and his colour began to return. Billy felt a little put out though because he was the last to get back his chunk. Feel-

ing like Indian givers, but knowing Stooky had had his supper at least, we closed our mouths glumly on our lumps
and retired for the night.

After rolling the unsweetened wads around our mouths
for awhile, we sadly wrapped them around the old bedstead,
hoping we'd at least dream tonight that we were still going
away, where gum grew plentiful and free.

Pa's Rubber Boots

◦◦◦◦◦

Pa's rubber boots were ancient, size eights, and the purest of rubber. He kept them in a small closet for rainy days and floods. The rule was we were never to go near those priceless boots unless Pa was drowning, or unless he was thrown out of a plane and landed on a high tension wire.

However, when Pa was hundreds of feet under the good Lord's earth in the coal mine, Billy would take his chances, considering first the time it would take Pa to land back on the surface and, secondly, how fast he could make it back to the closet with Pa's boots. Billy looked very proud wearing those boots, but I wouldn't even chance wearing them today, and Pa's been dead for thirty-five years.

One fall day a monsoon started with torrential rains. There were small ponds of water everywhere. The idea of building a dam came to Billy. In order to engineer the job, he had to have rubber boots, and what better opportunity to wear Pa's boots, with him at work. So Billy, wearing the boots, automatically became the foreman. He'd shoot out an order standing in two feet of water and our eyes would come to rest on Pa's boots. We knew we had to obey him because anyone brave enough to wear Pa's rubbers was capable of overseeing the digging at the ruins of Pompeii while the volcano was still erupting.

Barefoot, the rest of us helped by getting material for Billy: sods of dead grass, cowflaps and flat stones, which would also come in handy to bury Billy in the event Pa caught him wearing his boots. Soon we had stilled many cubic feet of water and were thinking of starting a hydroelectric dam, but it was near evening and we knew Pa would be home shortly, so Billy left for the house to put the boots back. Suddenly Billy dropped to the ground. We peered in his direction. Our worst nightmare was in the picture – Pa. We could see him strolling around the yard in his bare feet, and his wide police braces, with only one brace holding up his size forty-four pants, while the other brace swung leisurely unshouldered. If it had been one of us going around in this state of disarray, Pa would have instantly charged us with vagrancy and indecent exposure.

Had we known the manager of the mine, he could have helped us considerably by sending up smoke signals to warn us that Pa was going to arrive early. The only way Billy could get out of this predicament, short of running straight up to Pa, clutching him by the shirt, and telling him a terrifying tale of how a crazy person had busted in, held him at gunpoint, and insisted he wear Pa's boots, was to sneak out to an old shed that housed all kinds of discarded odd rubber boots (which we'd gathered from the shores all year round to start our coal fire) and leave Pa's boots there. So Billy held his ground until Pa wandered into the house, and then he beat it for the shed, as though Vesuvius was erupting around him.

Later that evening, our old stove seemed sulky and draughtless, as though asking for something to spark it up. My turn to be fireman, I made for the shed, reached in at random, took two rubber boots and proceeded back to the house. On a smoky day, the old stove seemed to grin when it saw you with a rubber boot or two heading for its covers. Applying them one at a time, in a few minutes the stove was sizzling red.

Next morning after Pa had made his trek to the mine,

Billy went out to the shed to make the needed replacement and put Pa's boots back in his closet in the exact position he had found them. Opening the old shed door, he reached in expecting to capture Pa's boots. But in the spot where he had placed them, he came up with only one. Billy was seized with panic, thinking "My Lord, my Lord, be with us during our hour of bootlessness." A hundred old boots were scrutinized in minutes, but Pa's with the star on the sole was nowhere to be seen. Billy wondered for a second if he could blame it on the stove, and tell Pa that the stove had gone into the closet and come back with one of his boots to burn.

An urgent meeting was called. (Some weeks we had more meetings than Pa.) Teedy suggested we burn down the house, but this wasn't seconded because we knew Pa had no money for another one; and we would probably have ended up living out the rest of our lives in the outhouse. Our flour barrel and salt fish barrel could have fit over each of the holes, but where would we have fit the icebox? And a place that small wouldn't help us hide from Pa in an emergency, unless we held our noses and slid down the hole. And even that could only have been done when Pa's back was turned, because Pa had eyes in the back of his head, the side of his face, and probably on the soles of his feet. Our goose was cooked, and we couldn't even eat it.

In desperation we again rummaged through all the old boots, but no luck. We felt we were fortunate just to have *one* of his boots. Unfortunately we didn't know a good surgeon who would amputate Pa's left leg while he was sleeping, so he wouldn't ask for the left boot.

We prayed for dry weather and God was good and answered our prayers. Pa didn't use his boots for the whole long cold season. In the meantime, his single boot, looking chilly and lonely, peered up at us from his darkened closet, as if to say, "Does he know yet?" We were scared to go to the closet at all, in case the one boot jumped out at us and charged off to tell Pa.

As spring approached, we took that cold lonely boot out of the closet, and waited for the day of reckoning. We had a couple of last-ditch stories up our sleeves to spring on Pa if he accused us. One was that we would tell him there were rumours of a boot thief in town, who stole everybody's rubbers, melted them down and made tires out of them; and that Pa's rubber boots now graced the feet of a Model A Ford. Another alibi was that Teedy had surprised a ghost one morning in Pa's closet trying on his boots, and that it only had time to put one on before it vanished, boot and all, right up through the attic.

When the spring rains began, Pa made his way to the boot closet, our heartbeats in tune with each footstep. When he came out, our hearts skipped a beat, when we heard him saying with sad affection, "I must have left my old boots at the mine shed last fall. Well, it's time I had a new pair anyway." Eight ears shot straight up like donkeys and it took a lot of self-control to keep from giving Pa a great big hug, after which he would have had us all placed in a psychiatric ward, as no one hugged Pa, not even his mother.

Mothballs and Snuff

◦C◦C◦C◦

The most mysterious part of our house was a darkened corner of Pa's bedroom, close to the big clothes closet, where his locked trunk stood. For years we wanted to get into this trunk. It was like looking for buried treasure in Aladdin's cave, and it gripped our imagination more than chewing gum and our trip to Boston.

Two wide leather straps kept it tightly closed with the buckles snapped back to the last holes. A small oval key fit the ancient lock on this antique trunk. How we longed to get hold of that key, just for a little while, but we didn't know where to find it. We knew that Pa's unspeakable treasures were inside that trunk, maybe even the Hope Diamond, which we could have pawned for some gum. There was no way he was going to keep us from them, unless he took the trunk to the mine with him and buried it there.

Once, we got a quick peak inside when the lid was up, as Pa was looking for our birth certificates (he couldn't believe so many of us were born). But he had made sure we never got a sweeping glance and hurried us out of the room.

We had taken about as much of this secrecy as we could stand. So a search party was formed. We came to the conclusion that we shouldn't call in the police to help us search for the key, but we did think about asking an old man we knew, who was supposed to be psychic. We even tried to get our dog, Prince, on the case, but he couldn't smell out the keys unless they were hidden under an old bone. We searched for weeks and weeks for the key and came to the conclusion Pa must have swallowed it or given it to the mine manager to keep for him.

Nowadays we would have suggested Pa take Yoga lessons, and when it came time for the headstand, three of us could have balanced him on his head. Then Teedy could have lain on the floor, facing him and mumbling something to him, keeping his surprised attention, while Murray shook his pockets and Billy and I watched for the key to drop.

After hunting everywhere, Billy finally found the key. It was in a small cow horn on a nail above Pa's dresser. Right at the bottom of the horn, way underneath wads of wool and pills, nestled that little key. Now Pa would have no more secrets from us.

Our snooping started one day as soon as Pa left the house, while Ma was visiting a neighbour. The four of us crept up the stairs. Billy, grasping the key, approached the trunk like an Egyptologist. Silence reigned. Slowly he turned the key in the lock. A dog howled in the distance. The lid creaked open. Eight eyes peered over the rim and into the depths of the trunk. This had to be the quietest moment we had ever witnessed in our lives. At this point, Teedy suggested we wear gloves so they couldn't trace our fingerprints, because for a crime as bad as this, we knew Pa would employ Scotland Yard. But Billy thought the socks we wore for gloves would only be a hindrance.

Inside the trunk, under our very eyes, were foreign coins, a slipper, post cards, love letters, important legal documents, baptism papers, mothballs, rings, necktie clips, cufflinks, report cards, odd socks and a ring of keys.

Our first move was to take a coin each from the many that were there in an old cigar box. Each of us put an ancient coin in our pocket, then pulled it out again to have one more good peek at it, to get the date fixed in our minds.

We had steamy conversations about who owned the oldest and most valuable one, and what we were going to do with all our new-found wealth. Later on we tried to buy candy with them, but the woman who ran the store threw us right out, along with our coins.

In the bottom of the trunk were the baptism certificates of all twelve kids, and a very pretty scroll, with twenty or more baby pictures on it. We looked them over, each brother trying to pick out the picture that looked like him. There was only one baby picture that was cute, and each one of us claimed it was his baby picture. Then there were old pictures of our grandmothers and aunts and uncles, with their flattened-down hair and handlebar moustaches (even our grandmother). We read old post cards from the U.S.A., and Pa's love letters. We played with a railroad watch that weighed every bit of five pounds. And had Billy not tied a wet knot in the necktie he used for a belt around his waist, he would have been dragged to the floor, pants and all, from the weight of that watch. Billy actually sniggled this watch to school one day and told the kids the time about every two minutes, whether they wanted to hear it or not.

Next, our eyes fell on a small tin box. We'd heard Pa tell about a can of snuff a German prisoner had given him, many years back. We didn't know what snuff was, but had heard conversations that it was used for smoking or chewing. So we decided to have a toot.

As Pa smoked a pipe, there were a half dozen or more around the house. We got four pipes with plenty of matches and our can of snuff. Each one could barely wait his turn to fill his pipe. Packing it tightly in the bowl, we lit up and puffed away peacefully. Things were going nicely for a while, until Teedy turned a sickly grey, complaining of a pain in his belly. The rest of us were kind of high on the stuff and couldn't get down to Teedy's dilemma, although his sickness was getting worse. As far as we knew, he might die, before we closed the trunk. Imagine saying to Pa, "Pa, the snuff never hurt us, but it snuffed Teedy out."

Complaining to us that his belly was getting "worsah," we sobered up a bit, and tried our best to relieve him of his sickness. Billy snuck down to the kitchen and came bounding back with the soda box and a pan to throw up in. Two good teaspoons of bicarbonate did it. Up flew everything, even a string. After Teedy got his wind, he said he felt much better. I guess the rest of us had tougher innards, as we filled our pipes a second time and had the same feeling as the Asian and his opium.

Tiring of the snuff, mothballs next appeared on our menu from the floor of the trunk. A mothball smell always reminded us of riches. So we were into them head over heels. I still don't understand why Pa had mothballs in the trunk because there was no clothing, and we were the only moths. But what a temptation it was to take one lick of a mothball, they looked so much like mints.

It's funny how the four of us loved the smell of mothballs so much. Murray sat on Pa's bed with as many as a dozen mothballs on his lap, smelling them two at a time. All of a sudden, he jumped off the bed crying. A mothball had gotten stuck in each nostril. Billy quickly threw him over the bed and hooked one out with his little finger, but he couldn't get the other one out. It must have travelled up near Murray's brain. Murray's eyes were full of painful tears and he said even one ear was sore. A quick inspection of the ear found there were no balls in it, but it was overwaxed to quite a degree.

Next came a three-minute session about what to do with Murray's nose. Pa'd know something was wrong, since he was crying, as big as his eyes were. One nostril was getting all puffed out and he said the smell was making him sick. We thought of every way to get rid of that mothball. We even went as far as to blow into his bottom eyelid.

We couldn't keep Murray's fingers away from his nose and we knew he was just pushing the mothball further up. Suddenly Billy threw a handful of snuff at Murray and made him sneeze. To our ears came the beautiful sound of a dampened mothball rolling across the floor. That put Murray on the right breathing track again, and after this episode, he turned against the odour of the balls forever.

In a few minutes Pa would be home, and everything had to be back in order, even to the key in the small brown cow horn. We did our best to put things back exactly the way we found them (minus the snuff and the coins). We were good at that. Everything as neat as a pin, we retired downstairs to the kitchen to meet Ma and a hard-working Pa facing four little burglars, who had just finished reading his love letter to Ma of years gone by. The smell of burnt snuff was still on our breath, and Teedy was still burping up soda and snuff, which was followed by a sick grey smoke and a putt putt noise (the same as a dirty motor would make), and Murray's nose was throbbing and still held the aroma of mothballs (at least the moths would steer clear of him).

But Pa never did catch on, nor did he catch us in his trunk, for if he had, we'd be in it today, in the same state as the ancient Egyptian mummies, well preserved, with a mothball in each ear.

The Night I Slept with Pa

◦◦○◦○◦○◦

At an age when my dreams were concentrated on sleeping with the opposite sex, our relatives came from the States one night, and I had the terrible misfortune of having to bed down with Pa. Pa hadn't seen his oldest sister for years, so it was only logical that he'd ask her and her two sons to stay the night. This we hadn't bargained on, or we would have at least washed our feet, and hid the pot.

The adults were talking over old times in the front room, while all the kids stayed in the kitchen. Time wore on. The big Ben's tick was loud. Nine p.m. and we knew the grown-ups would soon be out to push us off to bed. And then the voting would take place as to who and what was to sleep where.

We four brothers always slept together. I never wanted to sleep with anyone else, only my wife if I were to get married, or maybe a hen – I always liked hens. Now it was suggested that cousin Ken sleep with us. This brought a screeching reaction from Ken, saying, "I'd never sleep in the same bed with Andy, his feet are dirty." I don't know what kept me from smashing him right then, but I had to control myself, as he was Pa's sister's boy. Suppressing my rage, I went over to a lovely colourful jacket hanging up in the closet, and yanked a button from it.

As everybody discussed who would sleep in what stable, Pa's pronouncement rolled above the din of voices, "Andy will sleep with me." (Ma, my aunt and my little cousin

51

Rob were to sleep in one bed.) Shocked, I was rooted to the floor. A buzzing started in my ears, my legs felt like butter. I went into a five-minute coma. Why, I couldn't sleep with Pa! He was a total stranger. Pa was more to Ken than he was to me. Ken was Pa's sister's boy. I was Ma's boy, and Pa was only my father. Ken started playing up to Pa with Uncle Fred this and Uncle Fred that, in a laughing manner. I just pretended I didn't know the man Ma had married. I thought I should even change my last name. It would be like sleeping with a policeman you didn't know. What a revolting development.

While everyone was on his way to bed, Pa's torturous words came floating down the fifteen steps, "Are you coming to bed or not?" as I crept cautiously up the steps to the gallows. It was far from a wedding night; it felt more like a funeral – mine. In all my thirteen years I had managed to keep well out of Pa's way, except when ordered to appear before him for a stiff sentencing for a bad report card. Now here I was sleeping with him! It had to be a dream, and I prayed it was. But I knew I was trapped. Should I sleep with all my clothes on, including my shoes?

My brothers, choking to keep from laughing out loud, threw out a few sexy barbs about Pa just as he gave another bellow, "Come to bed." He needed his early rest. Not me; I could have stood up on a chair all night without swaying. Pa had to get up at 4:00 a.m. for the coal mine, and his habit all his life was to close the bedroom door. That, right there, was enough for me! Our door was ajar at all times. And what with the claustrophobia I had developed as a kid, I could die with even a tight sweater on. I would do more than die in Pa's room; I would probably be locked away in the local asylum forever, with no visiting privileges.

In a trance, I closed the door noiselessly behind me. It

was pitch black. Suddenly, Pa roared, "The pot is under the bed." I was terribly shocked and offended. I felt like saying, Pa watch your language, not dreaming he ever knew I used a pot, or would even discuss such a thing. Little did Pa know I wouldn't have used his pot, even if my bladder was leaking out my ear. But the message about where the pot was located turned into music to my ears. At least I wouldn't step in it.

Now I was forced to find the body in this Black Hole of Calcutta. There was no way I was going to feel around in the dark. With my luck I'd probably puncture one of Pa's eyes or touch parts of him that were out of bounds, figuring Pa was out of bounds to begin with. Summoning up my courage, I got out a weak whimper, "Back or front?" while I stood at complete attention. Now the bed was against the wall, and Pa was sleeping on the near side. "Back," came the tired reply. Trying to levitate four feet across the foot of the bed, without touching Pa, I found my grave. There was no way I was going to touch Pa before I died. I knew that whatever position I assumed at that second of touch-down, that that would be it until 4:00 a.m. I had turned to stone.

Pa's bed was four and a half feet wide, and he weighed two hundred and fifty pounds, measuring an axe handle across the shoulders. I was a hundred pounds and measured a large foot across the shoulders, so I gave him plenty of room to lay his axe. I slipped into my pillar-of-salt state with a good foot between Pa and me, so I wouldn't be crushed flat as a cow plop on this cold and sad bedstead.

Pa was soon snoring away, leaving me with bedclothes the size of a handkerchief. Even though I was freezing to death, I didn't dare pull the bedclothes that covered Pa's huge frame toward me. It was as though I was lying beside a blanket of acid. If any portion of my body touched it, in seconds I'd be eaten up, or disintegrate in human spontaneous combustion. I'd have been better off sleeping in the clothes closet hanging on a nail. Pa's snoring turned into a foghorn. I felt like Daniel in the Lion's Den.

At one point I dozed off for about an hour, and I dreamt of the time Murray and I rolled the hydro pole all the way home, pushing it with our feet. Suddenly I woke up with both my feet in Pa's armpit, just ready to push him off the bed. All I needed was for him to wake up and find my big toe in his mouth. With the delicacy of a bomb-disposal expert, I eased my feet back and resumed my paralyzed position – in a state of rigor mortis.

When I next woke up in Pa's crypt, I figured it just had to be morning, but finding it was completely dark, I figured there was either an eclipse of the sun right in Pa's room or I'd gone totally blind. Palpitation took over instantly. Easing over Pa's body, I picked my way to what I thought was the door to the hall, but unknowingly ended up right in Pa's clothes closet. As I came in contact with three walls, my heart slowly stopped. Where in the name of God was I? Was I still asleep and having a nightmare, or had I slipped into some kind of a time warp where I was to be imprisoned forever? Was this a trick our house ghosts were playing on me, called "Let's scare Andy to death"? I knew I'd soon be among the realms of the deceased because I was gently smothering to death.

I could have been in Pharoah's tomb. I began clawing the walls in a kind of sickly way. I was trying to save my breath in case the oxygen ran out. I was still scratching weakly at the walls, when Pa suddenly burst onto the scene. "Mother of mercy," he cried, "what are you doing in here?" He lit a match and it was the first time in all the years I'd known Pa that I was glad to see him. I even tried to shake his hand. I know that if Pa hadn't arrived at that very second, my family would have been relating the story for years, saying, "Andy must have walked in his sleep and we didn't even know it. We found him dead upstairs in the closet, and the only conclusion we could come to was that rather than sleep with Pa, he smothered to death in the closet."

As it was near to 4:00 a.m., Pa decided to get ready for the mine. Once he got out and was on his way to the kitchen, I relaxed, took a long awaited turn back in bed, coughed myself inside out, and scratched every place that itched. I was shortly awakened by "goodbye and come again," under Pa's window. Taking a peek out the window to make sure Ken was leaving with my relatives, I thought next time these cousins wouldn't get such good treatment. I'd spray the place with flytox, and as they were coughing and sneezing, they'd blame it on the weather and leave.

It was very warm in Pa's bed, and my eyelids got heavier and heavier while I was thinking: never again will I sleep with Pa, if I have to stand upright in the fireplace all night, or if the only available bed left is a row boat.

Our Pet Fly

◦C◦O◦O◦

One fall day, while the rest of the class were busy studying history, Murray and I, sitting together at the same desk, were being bored to death as usual. So Murray started shooting spitballs with an elastic band. Interested in his remarkable skill, I kept my head close to him to avoid the history lesson, and would peek up every now and then to check for the teacher.

Murray was on a hunting expedition. Whispering real low, he said, "See that fly on the book. Watch how close I come to it." Murray took his aim and we suddenly had one of the seven wonders of the fly world. The fly dropped on our desk with its rear end completely severed from its body, almost as though we'd used a precision knife. But the accident didn't seem to affect the fly in the least – except for the fact that it couldn't fly, even though its wings were still in perfect shape. It didn't have any place to go anyway.

So while the rest of the class were mumbling about kings who'd died from gout and ague, we were teaching ourselves science, with the specimen running around on our desk. We took our pencils and succeeded in fencing in the fly. It didn't take much of a fence to hold it. I believe the shock of the spitball hitting it so suddenly had brought on the fear of climbing, because it didn't even try to climb once during its imprisonment. The next thing we needed for it was a house. A small oval pencil sharpener was the ideal home for our fly. It walked in the entrance, made a complete turn, came back to the front door of the pencil sharpener, then wiped its feet together and looked back over its shoulder as if contented.

That fly had more get up and go than those flies that buzzed around our windows all day in the sun. Murray and I wondered why they had to carry all that extra weight in the rear-end section, because our rearless specimen was almost as active as Murray and I – the only difference being, it couldn't fly and we could. It had lost that advantage in life. But so what? We lost advantages too when Pa saw our report cards.

Studying the fly's handicap, we were surprised to learn the things it could do. It held its front legs solid to the desk and clicked its two hind legs together, as if it were trying to knock a hair off its hind foot. Why couldn't the teacher have said, "Class, put your history books away now and let's study the fly's parts, which are head and thorax, with no abdomen. You probably don't know this, class, but Murray and Andy are Fly Tologists."

Sneaking our eyes up every now and then to see where the teacher was, we both had the same thought: we'd take the fly home, even though there were two or three sticky fly catchers hanging from the ceiling with some dead flies stuck to them and still kicking. There were still lots of flies beeping around the house. In fact, just a few nights before, Teedy had been taken by surprise while eating a hot bowl of soup, when a fly catcher over his head dropped and fell right into his bowl. Teedy told us he thought Pa had thrown an old necktie at him.

But this fly was special. Feeling badly about its accident, we were going to raise it as our own, even if we had to pack our two shoes and leave home. Why, this intelligent, bumless creature might have gotten us into Barnum and Bailey's Circus, if only we could have placed a bridle over its head. Of course one of us would have had to steer him.

We watched every step it took as it walked across the desk, stopped, threw its front legs up and rubbed them together. I whispered to Murray that it was washing its face or telling a joke about how it threw another fly out of the house one night. Murray just had to laugh and just a little too loudly. We were both so interested in our discovery that neither of us heard the teacher approaching with the pointer (which was hardwood, about half an inch in circumference at the small end, and nearly an inch at the handle). Our heads were still stuck close together and I don't know which part she swung down on our heads, but she got a bull's eye – the two of us at once.

That quickly broke up fly-keeping, but our biggest shock wasn't the smashing she'd given us, but the fact that she knocked a heavy history book smack on top of what was to be our bread and butter in the circus world. After the teacher retreated to her desk, Murray gently lifted the book to find that our pet was no longer much to look at unless you liked to look at a half-squashed raisin. Its wings were spread and its legs sprawled out like small hairs. Murray thought it was dead. But I knew it wasn't and I made a valiant attempt to resuscitate it (if your hearing was keen and everything was quiet around, you could still hear a small heart beat). The teacher was furious and said, "Why aren't you fellows studying?" While all this raving was going on, I placed Mr. Fly in a small change purse I had. I loved that fly and I was taking him home.

Now to Murray, it didn't make any difference as to how he talked to teachers. As far as he was concerned, they were just big pupils, like his eyes. So it was no surprise to me when he looked right into her beady eyes and said, "You just killed our fly." She turned all purple at this and we thought she was going to swear – and we kind of wished she had, so we could tell Pa on her. "Both of you, take your books and go home." Nothing could have been sweeter to our ears, as we picked up a few books and headed for the door.

Outside in the fresh air, Murray got a big surprise when I opened my change purse to air out our fly. Almost as good as ever, except for a slight limp, there it was, walking around the purse on an old key. "Good," I said to Murray, "still kicking." We slowed our walking pace because we didn't want to get home before school had been dismissed. Stopping at a small brook, we almost forced the fly to drink. My change purse became its headquarters as Murray threw in a few pieces of grass for it.

Finally, school was let out and we were free to roll along home with the other school kids. Ma was busy making a currant cake when we arrived. Secretly, we showed our fly to Ma, and she said, "Now, don't you fellows be cruel, and for heaven's sake, don't let your father see you with that fly." We got permission from Ma to get an empty biscuit box for its new home. The box was larger than my change purse and the fly could now exercise more.

We put in little dabs of molasses and wet bread, while the fly threw its two front legs up over its head and rubbed them together like it was knocking mud off its boots. We had something that was miraculous and we hated to leave it as we got ready to do the chores for the night. We asked Ma if we could leave it on the chair beside her until we were finished. "Put it there," said Ma, "but make sure it's out of here before your father comes home." We couldn't get the coal and wood into the house fast enough so we could return to our pet fly.

Pa would be home in ten minutes, so we rushed in and made for our fly. But there was no one at home in the box, except a few dabs of molasses and a wet piece of bread. "He's gone," we murmured sadly as Ma finished putting her cake in the oven. Shaking her head, she said, "There are enough flies around here now, without you bringing more home." But she knew we were broken-hearted. We searched all over. We didn't need a description; we'd never get it mixed up with other flies. Our fly bore no rear. We hunted cautiously through every room, as though it was a dangerous beast that had to be stalked.

Finally, after many minutes of looking, we knew our hunt was in vain, until Murray suggested we look upstairs, because he said he'd heard a strange buzz. Our other flies never sounded like that. While we were upstairs, Ma called us to supper, but it was Pa's alto voice that drew us downstairs instantly with one holler.

We were having fish cakes, crisped in bacon grease, potatoes and white currant cake. Murray and I ate slowly, but we didn't feel hungry, and we took odd peeks at the ceiling. Pa was talking about some miner's wife having the flu while he picked up a piece of hot cake. Holding the piece of cake in his hand for some time to make his point, Murray and I spied a rare phenomenon. Pa was eating our fly. We were speechless. Had Pa looked at either of us, he'd have thought we had died sitting up. If we didn't halt Pa's next bite, we'd see the last of our remarkable, educated, scientific fly. But it was too late. Pa had downed the cooked fly. Saddened by this turn of events, we felt like we should give the fly a hero's funeral – but we would have had to bury Pa along with it.

Run for Your Life

◦◦◦◦

About once a year in the spring, Pa would get up the energy to make repairs to the two little outhouses we had on our property. But our old handsaw was usually dull after a winter of hitting nails, sawing up old boards for kindling. Now, Pa knew an old black man who lived about two miles from home, and he was a corker at sharpening saws for only a quarter. This day Pa picked me as the ambassador to take the saw to him.

Pa told me, "If Jim isn't home, just tell his wife who you are, and what you want done." Well, that wasn't hard to remember. I was to go in the early morning, before nine, so I would catch Jim. Talking about it that evening, I asked a neighbour of ours if it would be hard to find the place. "No, you won't have any trouble, Andy. The house has bars over the window upstairs. They keep a crazy woman there. Nobody's seen her for years." At twelve years of age, I wasn't too brave, until Ma said, "Oh, don't worry about her. She's locked upstairs, and she's four times your age." Those comforting words from Ma made me walk straighter, without a worry in the world. With the saw in my hand, and permission from Pa to wear my Sunday shoes, I strutted along quite sexy, whistling "Sentimental Journey."

Nearing my destination, Ma's reassurance began to fade like a sunset. With a lump in my throat, I lifted my head and focused my eyes on the dark barred window upstairs. But I remembered what Ma had said. Nothing for me to worry about. It was now 10:00 a.m. and a beautiful day. Chasing the fears from my mind, I opened the gate and sauntered up to the door. Did the gate sound like a foreboding voice when it closed, or was it just my imagination?

I knocked on the door as a large black crow sitting in a lifeless tree cawed and shook its feathers at me in a dark kind of way. I thought I could hear it say, "Leave this place." I'd now forgotten why I'd come to this house. My mind raced for an explanation to give the gentleman or lady who would answer my knock. What was I doing here? The saw, it must be the saw. I must have found it and was now returning it. Suddenly, with my mind still a blank, the door burst open. All my greatest fears were immediately realized in the menacing dark form that hovered in the doorway.

The hairs on my body stood up and the skin on my face began to shrivel. I'd arrived at the gateway to Hell. A black turbaned mammoth of a woman, encased in coins and beads like a witch doctor, laughed hysterically at my shrinking twelve-year-old frame. I wondered what death at her hands would be like, but I knew I would die before I found out. Then before I could say Jack Robinson, a huge fist ripped through the air, and with one breath I was yanked inside. Even in the jaws of death I remembered the saw. It was Pa's saw. I'd fight to the death for Pa's saw. Why, I might even have to use it to save my life. Struggling in her mighty grip, the end was near; she was about to devour me, but then, like a miracle, she let go of me to change her grip, and like a bullet I was gone down the path and through the gate.

No gazelle on earth could have matched my pace as I headed for wide open space – a field by her house. But she must have been an antelope in another life, because when I glanced over my shoulder, to my horror, she was only a few yards behind. Like a train, she roared down the tracks of death after her prey. The coins and beads rolled like waves across her chest, to and fro, to and fro, as the huge engine picked up steam. I was running so fast the saw should have sharpened itself with all the wind whistling through it.

She was running straight out now, and the hideous laughter grazed my ears like a sharp frigid wind. She must have had a great sense of humour. Was I that funny? I couldn't think of anything to even smile about. I ran in a zigzag fashion, and so did she. I'd dart to the left and dart to the right, and so would she. She was gaining on me, so with one last-ditch effort, I gave a mighty push and, with feet churning like propellers, came the closest to flying I've ever come. Then she began falling behind out of sight. After three trips around the field I'd beaten her. Now I could stop and breathe and get my bearings. There was a small pond, forty feet square, at the lower end of the field. I must have lost her there, but I'd have to take another route home – I didn't want to go back by her place.

Unwinding my tight muscles, I was much more relaxed after my breather. I walked leisurely along toward home. Just wait until I got hold of Ma! Suddenly I stopped. I listened. Was it my imagination, or did I hear snorts? Had she crept up behind me, or had she become invisible to suddenly reappear now and rip me to shreds? I wheeled around and there before me was a large, black horse. Lord above she'd changed her form, she'd become a Hell-horse! The horse snorted again, and then it charged. I sprung for the pond. Ducks in a group applauded my efforts as I streaked through the water like a mallard. I was now forced back to her house. There was a wire fence on the other side of the pond. That was my target. Heading for freedom – freedom. Suddenly, frenzied laughter filled the air, and out from behind some leafless alders, beads and coins swishing and jangling around her neck, lunged Mrs. Hell. It was like all the demons from the bottomless pit were unleashed upon the few square inches of earth I stood on.

I almost made it through that wire fence without the help of my hands, and it was four feet high. Safely on the other side of the fence, still holding Pa's saw, I was brave but tired, and now shoeless. The soft mud in the pond had claimed my Sunday shoes. My next run would be escaping from Pa. Hell-horse, back on the other side of the fence, rearing and snorting, had a look as though to say, "Well if you lost your two shoes, I'm not taking any chances losing my four."

The horse looked at the crazy woman and gave a sharp whistle through its nose. She glared at it, shrieked and gave a blood curdling laugh. That was enough for the horse and me. He galloped off and I took off for home, as she skipped back to her house, jangling and tittering all the way.

When I arrived home, Ma was all smiles and said, "Well good, Jim sharpened it while you waited, did he?" I said, "Hold on Ma, it's not sharpened and I lost my shoes." After telling her about my adventures over the past two hours, she had to laugh. She should have been back there with Mrs. Hell. They could have laughed themselves sick. But when Pa arrived, Ma never mentioned my brush with death, in case Pa decided to make a trotting horse out of me.

"Well," Pa said, "I forgot poor Jim has been in the hospital, with ulcers, for the past two weeks and the crazy daughter's mother has a job to go to each morning, until noon."

We found out later that after feeding her unbalanced daughter that morning, Jim's wife had forgotten to lock her in. So all the strength, wind, speed and laughter that she had bottled up was unleashed on me after many months of imprisonment. I suppose it was therapeutic in a way that she was able to get rid of some of it during her work-out.

As for me, I was now ready to enter the sprints at the next Olympics.

So after dinner, my three brothers and I, lugging a hoe and a rake, soon retrieved my slippery little boots in the pond. We then beat it for home, wearing strings of garlic and large crosses around our necks, and carrying sharpened wooden stakes, just in case we were accosted again by Hell-horse and Mrs. Hell.

Tell Pa I'm Dead

∘C∘O∘O∘

Professional baseball was played in our town, years before the Second World War. We four brothers, in our early teens, would wait until the games ended and the spectators had left the stands. Then, along with about ten guys our age, we'd go around the field and pick up all sizes of cigarette butts, and have a great time after dark, smoking our own.

It would have been curtains if Pa had ever smelled nicotine on our breath. So after a good puff, we'd go to the pasture, chew some grass and swallow it just like a cow. We found that it really took the smell off your breath. And anyone who had a greenish tint to his teeth had to be one of our pals who'd been puffing.

One Saturday evening, I picked up a broken pipe of Pa's – just the bowl, no stem – and I decided to get some cigarette butts, open them up, relax, and get a good big pipeful to smoke. It was damp and humid this evening, and the butts were heavy and soggy, but I continued stuffing them into the pipe. All alone, I sat at the top of the grandstand: my look-out post. You could look over the fence to see if Pa or the police were coming.

My pipe's extra large bowl was soon loaded. I lit match after match, but could barely puff to get it going. As I lit more matches, I realized I had packed the bowl too tight. The thing must have stogged along the short, broken stem to the bowl. I prepared for one good blow to clear it, not realizing the bowl would be dead level with my eyes. With the largest blow ever made by man or typhoon, I blew through the tightness as if I was trying to inflate the Hindenburg. The tobacco flew right into my eyes, with all the fire on top. I was blinded. I staggered around, clutching at my eyes, and with one bad step I toppled right off the grandstand, plunged to the ground, and struck my head on a pop cooler.

I don't know how long I was there, but when I woke up, I was lying on an old door in the back of a half-ton truck. The next thing I heard in my semi-coma was Pa saying, "Where did you find him?" and then Pa humming "Abide with me." Without flicking an eye lash, I was beginning to remember a few things. My foggy head had to figure out a perfect alibi. The pipe, Pa's pipe, was over near the grandstand. I thought if they take Pa over there to show him where I fell, they're bound to see the pipe. Listening to a conversation about myself, and me dead in the back of a truck, was quite disturbing. But Pa continued to ask questions, thinking I'd been clubbed to death. My three brothers' voices came to my ears, and I could hear their surprise. "We were with him after the game. He was all right then."

As we began the trip home I felt like a pretzel, bent, twisted and half eaten. I then thought about shocks. This truck didn't have any. Every time it rumbled over a bump, I was thrown to a different part of the truck box. The fall from the stand hadn't killed me, but the truck ride might. The headlines would read, "Boy jarred to death in truck."

You would have thought that Pa could have sat back there with me and restrained my jumping frame. But then again perhaps he had more important business up front with the driver. Maybe they were discussing yet another upcoming union meeting. The next thing I knew, we must have struck the granddaddy of all bumps, because in one motion I was lifted and hurled from the truck onto the road.

I was left mangled in the dust, with the truck roaring out of sight. A bird flew over head; it glided sofly through the sky. I prayed it wasn't a vulture. Laying there gave me much time for reflection. I came to the conclusion that all union meetings, grandstands, broken pipes and trucks without springs should be banned from the face of the earth.

It seemed that weeks passed. In a daze, I tried to figure out why it was taking them so long to come back and find me. Pa and my brothers had to be searching for me. What good would my funeral be without my body? Then it occurred to me why I was still there – Pa and the truck driver had been rolling along discussing meetings. Then as Pa looked back and realized my body had been flung from the truck, they had started to wheel the truck around, when a man on the road, yelled, "Stop!" Then this man must have told Pa about the lack of food in the forest for the birds and animals. With tears in his eyes, he probably begged Pa to leave my body behind so that the animals and birds might not go hungry. No doubt Pa would agree. Then the truck driver would agree, and my brothers too. That's why I was still here.

Before I could come up with another explanation for being stranded so long, I heard a motor in the distance. For the first time in my life I longed to see Pa's face. I was soon rewarded. It was Pa, the truck driver and my brothers. Pa bent over to pick me up and carried me to the truck. This time I sat in the front. We began our trek home again.

When we got home, Pa kept a sharp eye on me for awhile, until Billy told him that I'd be better off alone without anyone bothering me, as I still wasn't all there. Thankfully, it was only a few minutes after that that Pa took to reading his evening paper. We still had to come up with an alibi.

Billy waited until Pa got real interested in the paper,

then snuck me something up to wave off the odour of the tobacco – in case Pa decided to give me the last rites. Pa was a great smeller and I hadn't had time to get to the pasture for fresh grass. Later on, we let Pa believe that my near-death came about because I wasn't used to heights, took a bad spell, and toppled over. Billy, who could convince Pa that the earth was square, told Pa that he was with me one time when I climbed up two rungs of a ladder, took an attack of vertigo and fell into his arms – it was all he could do to revive me.

Teedy told Pa that sometimes when I was going up the stairs to bed, at about the ninth step, I'd begin to take dizzy spells, and he always stayed close behind me just in case. Then he'd sort of push me up the rest of the stairs until I recovered from my elevation fears.

Murray went right along with their stories, telling Pa that once when I was with him at the grandstand, I got to the top seat and just froze. He had to get three men to carry me down blindfolded.

Pa was really thinking things over now, and kind of feeling sorry for all the times he'd sent me up those steep stairs to bed, alone. So after Pa thought about my new phobia for a while, my sentences were confined to the first floor from then on.

I smoked a pipe in later years, but you can be well assured the bowl was at least eight inches from my face, the tobacco dry, with Pa living in a different house than me so that I wouldn't have to chew any more grass.

Honey Child

◦◦◦◦◦

The admission to get on the baseball field when we were young and penniless was fifteen cents for Juniors. We loved baseball, and if we were asked we would help fix up the field the day of the game, liming it for a free ticket. Kids living farther away had no chance to do this work, as we were only hired because we were closest to the park. It seemed I was always lucky in getting the various jobs, like water boy, ball boy or bat boy.

Now there was this well-known athlete and store owner who would come to all the games from Sydney, and he'd have an armful of scorecards that he'd sell on the grandstands, at ten cents each. Well, it turned out that he gave me this job. Was I important selling those cards! I was the envy of all the other kids.

Before each game started, this man would drive up in a late model car and ask a kid or two if they knew if honey was around. Well, believe it or not, that's what he called me. I didn't care what he called me, as long as I could make a penny. He'd laden me up with scorecards before the game, with change for a dollar. I was to get fifty per cent of the sales; one card cost a dime. I'd sell them in no time because miners aren't cheapskates. They'll buy anything that goes with the game. Loading me up with cards, it was honey this, and honey that. "Now that you're all set honey, I'll be back later." But he never came back. He'd get stone drunk, and they had to deliver him back home to Sydney, eighteen miles away.

This one day, I had six dollars of his on me. He only came by once a week, so what was I to do with his money for a whole week? I didn't open my mouth about the money to anyone. I had it mostly all in silver, in an empty jam bottle inside an old rubber boot, behind the outhouse. I almost went crazy trying to ignore my brothers' wants. They knew I was wealthy, but I refused to tell them where the loot was hidden.

The following week the man would do the same thing, and then the next and the next. He'd say, "Do your best honey, I'll see you," and off he'd fly to get drunk. Now here I was with twenty-four dollars all to myself, and him smiling and patting me on the shoulder. I wondered how long this would continue. I'd soon be able to buy the baseball park. Meanwhile, my brothers scanned the universe, searching for my treasure, not knowing that each day they were almost sitting on it, unless they were constipated.

An old black man wearing a long coat, with deep pockets full of pennies, would come by now and then for rags, iron, rubbers, and bones. We'd give him either a piece of iron, or a bone, and he'd reach down into that long coat pocket and give us a penny. Now, I had the jam bottle with my loot stuffed into the toe of the knee boot, and it was getting quite heavy. I had just sold the old man a few rags for a penny, when I spied Teedy passing the black man my rubber boot. The man tossed it onto his low wagon and Teedy reached out for his penny. I was always a little scared of the black man, but this time I jumped on his wagon, grabbed the rubber boot, and ran away with it, the old man tearing after me. When I saw that the black man was bound to keep running, I reached into the boot while running, retrieved the jam bottle, stuffed it under my sweater, and threw the boot behind me. The man stopped, mumbled a few words, picked up the boot, and returned to his horse and wagon. Teedy still didn't know why I had run away with the boot. He kept telling me it was full of holes, that it was heavy, and why would I want only one boot anyway. Well, there was one good reason. The boot with the bottle in it was worth twenty-four dollars, twenty-three dollars and ninety-nine cents more than Teedy had sold it for.

The day before the next baseball game, a shiny car pulled into our yard. A man got out and asked Pa if honey was home. Pa kind of moved out of his path, sort of on guard, in case he made a pass at him (it would have been his last pass). "Who are you looking for?" says Pa, "a male or female?" (hoping Ma wasn't running around on him, without him knowing about it). "Your boy, the one who helps me sell scorecards." "Why not call him by his first name, before people start getting ideas?" says Pa.

I was upstairs at the time. Pa stomps up after me, and says, "Do you know what it wants?" "Guess he wants me Pa," I said, as I ran downstairs and quickly walked my friend out of range of Pa's hearing, so Pa wouldn't know the huge amount of cash hidden on his property.

"Well honey, how did you do the past few weeks?" said the man. "How many did you sell?" "Well, all of them," I said, as he came so close to me I thought he was going to kiss me. For the last few weeks, I'd been hearing so much talk about him and "honey" from the rest of the gang, I was getting to the stage where I wouldn't dare turn my back on him, even if I had to lead him out the door. Suddenly, I yawned. It was the biggest, longest yawn I ever performed. I don't know if he thought I was tempting him or not, but he placed his two hands on my shoulder and said, "Honey, I got news for you." Thinking he was going to say, "Let's get married now, and we'll buy a small grandstand and raise little scorecards to sell," I was getting ready to holler "Pa" at the top of my lungs. Instead he said, "All I want is fifteen dollars. You're an honest kid. The rest is yours." I ran for a post hole where I now had my bottle covered up with a few dead leaves, like a squirrel's cache of nuts. All I could see was dollar signs, with the feeling I'd never have to work again. With such a good hiding place, every penny was intact. I legally had nine dollars.

The man was kind and honest and it was just that everyone was honey to him. But if he'd ever called Pa honey, I'd have had the full twenty-four dollars to keep. Pa would have clobbered him with one swing of his three-fingered hand, and the only trouble we'd have had then was to dispose of the poor honey man's body.

There's Money in Needles

◦◦◦◦◦

During the cold months the need for money grew. Somehow at this time a needle company picked up my name. I often wondered where on earth they got it. Maybe they got it off the truant officer's list, figuring Andy MacDonald's never in school. He'll have plenty of time to sell needles.

Anyway they sent me a catalogue in full colour with beautiful pictures of cameras, knives, popguns and scooters – which were their rewards for promptness. It was my job to sell forty packets of their needles at ten cents a packet. I was to keep a dollar for myself and send them three. With that Christmasy feeling starting in November, I could hardly wait to get started, so I sent away for all kinds of needles.

My first customer was Ma, and even though I gave her the needles on tick (credit), I still felt as though I'd just been made President of Fort Knox. My business venture was right up Billy's alley. Knowing his penchant for zeroing in on a deal like a bloodhound, I knew I'd have to have him as an employee. He was such a good salesman, he talked me into it. He'd take one of my packets, sell it on the way to the show and have four cents left over to spend like a drunken needle salesman.

Along with the needles, they sent little sachets of perfumed powder to be presented with each sale. I felt people were lucky enough just to get the needles, so I kept the powder for Ma and my sisters, who normally used oatmeal dust for powder. One time Teedy, Murray, Billy and I threw

74

several packets in our bath water and smelled like roses
for a week. Teedy said if we put the powder on Pa's hair
when he was asleep, it would bring good luck, like when
you put salt on a bird's tail. The only good luck we got was
when we were able to escape from Pa's room, after we tried
it, without getting killed.

Getting rid of the powder made it easier for me anyway, because now I only had the needles to contend with.
Selling over twenty packets, I was starting to get uppity. I'd
have sold snow drifts if there had been money in it. However, it wasn't long before I was taking a loan of a few pennies and not returning them to my bean can, which was
where I kept my needle money. My bean can did not runneth
over. And no wonder; Billy found it and visited it more often than Napoleon visited Josephine.

The days were getting colder and I began slackening
up on my selling. I'd let a week go by before I'd start an
all-out sales campaign. Inside that week, I would be liter-
ally robbed by Billy (and myself) taking packets to sell for
the show. We were living like extravagant kings. Billy should
have gotten a job with the drug squad. He'd have been terrific at sniffing out marijuana. No matter where I hid the
bean can, he found it. I believe he was psychic. Because he
knew each hiding place in the house, I decided to put a wire
through the can and hang it on a spruce tree way in next to
its trunk. We never got too close to this tree because wasps
nested in it. But one day Billy was throwing a stone at a
saucy crow and pinged the can. Not caring if the wasps
carried him into the next province, he climbed up and found
the needle money. Had there been astronauts in those days, I
could have gotten Armstrong to hang it on a corner of the
moon, but ten to one they'd have taken Billy as batman. I
couldn't take the can to bed with me. Billy slept with me.
About the only way I could see myself hanging onto that

money would have been to rent a locker in New York City.

Having access to all this money made people notice an independent air about me. How I got money to go to the show anytime baffled everyone, even me. But it was no trouble at all as long as Billy left me some needles. Since he was eating up my supply of needles, I presented him with two packets of powder. To my amazement, I found out later that he had sold these for ten cents. I suspected as much because he smelt the same as before I had given him the powder.

In a funny way, I didn't mind Billy taking my needles. It made him a partner to the guilt I was feeling. I also loved the authority that I had as the banker over Billy. And I couldn't have had a better guy in my corner, unless it was Al Capone – smiling all the time, yet undermining me so bad, I couldn't do anything else but fall.

Everyone was having a spree on me and I went right along with them trying to keep everyone happy. I took Teedy, the youngest, on an outing that would equal a trip to Disneyland today, and it only cost me two packets of needles. I can still see Teedy strutting along beside me, gum rubbers eating his woollen socks. The top of his sock was visible for a few struts, then it would vanish. The suction from the toe of the rubber boot would suck the sock to the toe in minutes, but Teedy would walk right along with a limp on the lump, knowing a candy was in the offing. When it came to candy, Teedy could have had both hands tied like Houdini and still have been able to put candy in his mouth, without sharing it. He was so proud of his brainy brother, the needle man (I even had the build of a needle from worrying about my money), he doted on everything I said and did, treated me like a king, and thought it quite fantastic when I sneezed or even wiped my nose, whether it needed it or not. He was having his first fling as a financier's brother, and I knew if a fight started, he'd be on my side or I'd leave him out of my will.

Everything had to be done on the sly. Pa didn't know I'd received the needles. He'd have thought I was becoming a seamstress, a witch doctor who stuck pins in voo-doo dolls, or a pin cushion. It's a good thing he didn't catch on or he would have laid me on a bed of needles like the holy men in India.

To this day, I would like to know why my family didn't support me in my business enterprise and why they didn't order forty packets of needles to keep the wonderful feeling going! We'd have been listed with the Rockefellers and the Astors in *Who's Who*, with a paragraph stating, "The MacDonald family gained their wealth in needles," showing a picture of Billy holding one sachet of powder and me with nothing but a sign saying "Sold out."

After a few more weeks, things began to run down hill. With three-quarters of the needles sold, and only thirty-seven cents in the cup, my ambitions were beginning to sour. The fleeting happiness of selling a packet, then escaping to the show, had finally worn off. Now things got serious. How was I going to pay back the company? I thought of suicide, but I'd have had to take Billy with me. Visions of languishing in debtor's prison went through my head and I wondered if Billy would accompany me. He could have bribed the judge with a package of powder.

I could think of nothing short of putting Pa's house up for sale. Of course Pa would go with the house. If it was all right with Billy, they could live together, and Billy could have Pa for a buddy. Also, I had my eye on the fire hydrant near our house, but after finding it cemented up, I decided I'd leave it for the dogs.

Billy of course had no remorse. I could see his point. He had nothing to show that he was once a needle man, not even a sprinkle of powder. In fact, he felt the company owed *us*. As I said before, it was the needle company's offer that if you sold the needles in thirty days, a reward was given for promptness. Boy, how I extended those thirty days. It ran into ninety days, with letters coming from the company saying they'd still allow me my extra gift for promptness. As I had no money to send in and very few packets of needles left, I wondered if they would accept *my* offer that they keep their gift for promptness, and in return forget I ever ordered any needles (or even used them to sew buttons on). Then maybe they would send me a nice letter saying it was good trying to do business with you. Instead, letters poured in for three months afterwards. Nervous and exhausted, wherever I went I could see the company's name, Novelty Needle Company, Ltd., written across the sky. Why the Lord didn't deliver me from my troubles with a miniature heart attack, I don't know. But He must have had a good reason. I probably owed Him some money for needles.

Billy was wondering how I'd deal with this outburst of letters. I had no alternative but to ignore each one. I was even thinking of investing in a post office box and throwing away the key (I'd have had to rent it with the leftover needles, but there weren't any left now). Six months later, the company was still writing, still willing to give me the thirty-days promptness gift if I sent in the three dollars.

After they'd spent four dollars on stamps, they gave up. I knew I was on their blacklist, that every employee in their company right down to the janitor knew who Andy MacDonald was. In fact, I don't imagine it would be safe for me to order those needles even today. And that's a pity. I've been thinking of practising acupuncture. But here again, I'd have to employ Billy because people have been wondering why he hasn't been sitting in his favourite seat at the show six days in a row every week.

Will the Real Twenty-six Please Stand Up

With all the strappings I received in school, the only reason I have full use of my hands today is because of the periods of rest they got during my days of truancy. This one particular morning, I had been sitting on a rock at the shore, with the waves washing all around me, listening to the sounds of the ocean.

No matter how long I stayed away from school, there always came a time when I had to return, just to put in an appearance so they wouldn't think I was dead. But I usually picked a dilly of a day. And this day was no exception. For some reason, probably because it had started to rain, I sat there listening to the screeching seagulls and made up my mind to go to school. Slithering off the huge rock like a merman, I had an inkling I was in for a bad day, but I didn't know how bad.

Back in school, everything looked new and smelly to me after coming from the wide Atlantic with each wave looking as if it knew me personally and the salt breezes whistling through the wound-up scribbler I used as a decoy in my back pocket. While I was away, they had even polished my desk with a light varnish. All shiny, it was as though my desk was trying to coax me to get in the groove and stick with the class.

A few weeks before our teacher had invented a new roll call. Instead of names, we went by numbers – just like prisoners. Mine was twenty-six. When a number wasn't answered, the teacher would ask if so and so was sick, who lived close by the kid, and all that craziness. She had stopped at my number so many days in a row for so long that number twenty-seven began to follow twenty-five. As far as I know, I don't think they even used twenty-six in arithmetic that entire year.

Now, once a year, unannounced, the Inspector of Schools would drop in, like magic, right out of the sky. Why he never picked a day when I was playing hookey made me think that J. Edgar Hoover had a file on me.

This day, I had just gotten settled in my seat when a weak, low knock came to the door. There was the devil himself! (We could automatically tell it was a male at the door because Mrs. Brindell would blush right through the back of her white crepe blouse. She was single, in her late forties, and any male with authority made her smile.) I could see that the viper at the door meant trouble for me. Over the threshold he stepped, a short, thin man with a pen in his hand and his left arm full of papers, ready for action. He had a mean look about him that struck terror into my heart. Mrs. Brindell placed a chair near her desk. He sat down, spread his papers all over the place, and looked as though he was planning the Spanish Inquisition.

Dropping myself into the lowest gear I could, I sort of slid under the desk, like a fish slipping off a hook, and began practising the art of becoming invisible. If you were at the front of the room, a quick glance would give you the impression my seat was vacant. I was hopelessly behind in my lessons on account of my truancy. I stayed crouched in this position, praying, "Don't ask me anything. I shouldn't be here anyway, but it's raining like heck outside now and my gum rubbers are leaking." Little did they know that I only came that day to dry my feet.

"Class rise," intoned our teacher. "This is Mr. Failin.

Now be seated." What a name! Right up my alley. I should have stood up right then and there, with my chest out, chin tucked in, and said to the Inspector, "Your friend there, hot lips, has been calling me Failin since I started school; and if you play your cards right, I can fix you up with her." She passed him the large register which looked like an over-sized report card. Sitting at her desk, he opened the huge book, while she fluttered around him in circles like a ruffled grouse, lifting her feet gently so as not to tamper with the air around his body. At odd times, she'd give a quick glance at the class. She couldn't see me. When she did eventually notice me, I expected her to say, "Mr. Failin, we have a visitor who only comes once in a blue moon. Try to be fair with him. He's a slow learner, a real lame brain, and he's way, way behind the rest of the class." And to plead my case even further, she could have told the man, "Why this boy has gone senile, and will soon be applying to the government for a pension." Time and time again, Mrs. Brindell told us how she had been humiliated by an answer I, or another stupid student, had given to the Inspector. Would this visit be different?

Now, Murray, my twin, sat behind me this year in school. But because of my extended absence, it was getting difficult to recognize him. However, he assured me we were brothers. Murray had a plan to make me appear as an example of how the education system could work. For the past few days, he'd been reading an advertisement about hypnosis and now thought he was Svengali. He said that when the Inspector asked me a question, no matter how difficult, I was to give him any old answer, even if I was totally wrong. How was this to be accomplished? Murray was going to hypnotize Inspector Failin! When asked a question, any answer I gave would be correct because Murray would *will* the Inspector to believe it was. If all else failed, there was a back-up plan. Murray would slouch behind me and give me the answer.

The Inspector began his search for information to my left, near the front of the room. I glanced at Murray behind me. He had begun his hypnosis. He glared at the Inspector, then squinted real hard. Next he hummed under his breath. After this, a soft "You're getting sleepy, you're getting tired, you're getting sleepy." I looked at the Inspector. He didn't seem too sleepy. He continued asking questions. Each kid he asked gave an answer he was pleased with, and each time the teacher beamed with pride.

I glanced at Murray. He was getting even more intense. His face was now a greenish colour, but he was still chanting, "Relax, relax, relax." Now came the supreme test. The Inspector had called up the stupidest kid in class, Grover. If Grover could answer the Inspector, I knew Murray's spell was working. Grover had never answered a question right in his life, not even what letter his name started with. A hush fell over the room. Grover stood up. I looked back at Murray. He was now purple. Although it was difficult to understand what he was saying, I think he was mumbling, "You are totally relaxed, and you will be quite pleased with Grover's answer." I looked over at Grover. He answered and the Inspector was tickled pink. Murray had done it! He'd actually hypnotized the Inspector.

My lowest gear still to the floor, the brakes pushed far in, I was motionless. I felt really safe until I heard a very deep voice in my direction. Number twenty-six resounded low and clear. Mrs. Brindell nodded at me, and gestured for me to stand. Sixty numbers! Why me, the best hid kid in the school? Gently turning on my ignition, and loosening my brakes, I slid to a standing position close to my desk. It would be a miracle if I knew the answer. But then I remembered Murray and the great spell he had woven around the

Inspector. Then came the question. I prayed Rasputin Murray's spell was still working.

"General Isaac Brock died on the battlefield. At what Heights was that?" droned the Inspector. Swiftly I chanced a backward glance at Murray. No help coming from that direction: he had hypnotized *himself* and was now slumped over his desk asleep! He couldn't even whisper the right answer to me. So I gave the Inquisition my answer. "The height of his career." A not-too-appreciative "Thank you" came from old Failin, while Mrs. Brindell made quick motions for me to sit down. They actually swapped a few snickering laughs before the next number was called. I retired to the position I had assumed before, out of sight. So much for hypnotism.

The next few numbers he called, I could hardly keep from jumping from my perch and shouting out the answers, as they seemed much easier. The class had come up with all the right answers and the Inspector was only seconds out the door, when the stately maid yelled, "Well, Andy MacDonald certainly didn't know the answer. We've had that lesson two days in a row now. Brock died at the Battle of Queenston Heights." It was a good thing I didn't have the right answer or she might have keeled over, and that wouldn't have looked too good in front of her skinny Romeo.

Mrs. Brindell took it for granted that everyone in the class knew the answer to my question. But I would have bet any money that Sam, two seats to my left, and a fine, stupid student, would have ended up giving a guess at General Brock's own height, five foot ten. After school, I practically had to drag Murray home. He was so totally relaxed, he could barely walk.

My penalty in class for days after that was to study the battle thoroughly, while the rest of the class continued on with a new lesson. I was so sick of Queenston Heights,

writing it over and over again on the board, that I was getting to the stage where I thought I was there and knew the
crazy general personally. That battle tormented my mind
night and day, so there was nothing for me to do but to
turn to truancy once again. I climbed back down the steep
cliffs to the shores. Those were my Heights. But I was much
luckier than Brock because I was never found dying there –
though I might have been if Pa had ever caught me.

Go Easy on Our Billy

◦◦◦◦◦

Then there were dentists. In particular, the time Billy paid his first visit to get one tooth filled and one pulled. We were deathly scared of dentists when we were young, and I am still scared of them today. It even scared us to look at the dentist's little white basin.

We used to cringe at the word "appointment." Instead of designating a specific time for your torture session, we prayed that the dentist would just say, "Drop in anytime when you are feeling brave. I'll even let you take all day to decide whether I should pull your tooth or not, and if you don't want it filled today, I'll take you out and buy you supper, and maybe we'll go for a swim."

We also felt that it would have made things a lot easier if each person in the waiting room were provided with ear plugs. Then we wouldn't have heard the patient in the chair giving out small groans. When we were actually in the chair, and the dentist put his drill down to go and mix his cement, we'd become quite brave. And it was an even more wonderful feeling if the phone rang when he was drilling. I'd pray that he would be held up on the line for two hours so I could catch up on my breathing. Once, when I was being worked on, the phone rang and I heard the dentist say, "Come right over sir." I displayed the first smile since dropping into that electric chair, thinking he'd begin on this man immediately – until he told me the caller lived fifty miles away.

This one time Pa had asked me to go with Billy to the dentist the next morning. We'd all be happy when Billy got his tooth out. Pa, my brothers and I were getting about a half hour's sleep each night. I think Billy was groaning, even when his tooth wasn't aching, just to keep the rest of us awake. And trying to keep Billy quiet was the same as trying to muzzle our salvaged cow. We tried everything for his sideless, backless tooth – soda, ginger, salt, a chew of Pa's MacDonald's twist, acupuncture, turpentine, shellac, dry stove polish – but nothing helped.

Tired and weary from nursing our patient, we were off to the dentist early next morning. I practically had to drag Billy to the building. Everything would have been hunky dory if the dentist's office had been on the first floor, but he was on the third. This guy, the oldest dentist in town and perhaps the whole world, was always quite busy. Many of his patients passed us on the stairway on their way out, holding a crimson rag over their mouth, some softly sobbing, and some holding teeth in their hands – a gift from the dentist to the tooth fairy. I tried my best to keep Billy on the inside wall, so he wouldn't see everyone who came down the stairs. And I felt quite proud that I was able to get him up to the third floor without him bucking.

Just as we entered the dentist's office, some kid was getting out of the chair, crying some, but in his right hand he carried an ice cream cone. Most dentists would give kids an ice cream cone, usually vanilla. But after an extraction, it turned to strawberry before you got down to the first floor.

The old dentist propped Billy up in the chair as I stood close by, like a midwife ready to deliver a child, while the dentist gave Bill his ice cream. Had there been an extra chair, I would have sat down as well to get a cone. Billy looked real happy with his chin all creamed up. "Now this won't hurt a bit," says the old, lying dentist, as he jabbed

Bill's gums full of novocaine. Billy had so much ice cream in his mouth that it wasn't much of a shock to have the dentist shoot some needles in. To further relax Billy, the dentist should have run back and forth from the torture chamber to the waiting room, regaling the death row inmates with dirty jokes. This would have served two purposes. It would have given Billy a breather, and would have taken the other patients' minds off the fate that awaited them. Also there was a good chance the dentist might have tripped and fallen during his race to and fro, knocked himself unconscious, and Billy would have been free to go home.

However, Billy soon started complaining to me about the funny way his lip felt. To ease his worry, I attributed it to the cold ice cream. But he looked at me as if to say, "It's not the ice cream, my lip has left my mouth." Then the old dentist walked into his secret stall, for his forceps. I wondered what he kept in that little room he darted into after giving Billy his needle. Was he laughing his head off at the size of Billy's mouth, or was he just waiting around in there having a smoke?

While keeping Bill's spirits up, I began to wonder why the dentist didn't keep his drills hidden. All he needed was an eight-by-eight-foot square built around the electric chair, with a small trap door behind him so he could reach for the drills. Why, I'll bet Billy would have been willing to build it himself. Once the enclosure was built, they could have then turned the radio up full blast so Billy couldn't hear the drill doing it's stuff.

The dentist returned from his closet and started chatting away. Why was he asking questions while his drill was in operation, and Billy cringing there with his lip puffed out with cotton batting, and a coat hanger buzzing on the side of his mouth to absorb the sewage? Instead, he should have hired a leprechaun to tickle the soles of Billy's bare feet.

Suddenly, the dentist accidentally dropped his forceps on the floor next to Billy. At first I thought Billy had dropped something out of his pocket. But this was Billy's big chance. He bounded from the chair, heading straight for the stairway with me in pursuit. As fast as he was going, he was still taking small bites off his ice cream cone. He never looked back. I used every muscle I had, but I was still yards behind him. It was almost a mile before he stopped to wait for me. "Take a look at my tooth," says Bill. "What did he do to me?" opening his mouth wide. His fenceless tooth still looked the same, and was ready to keep us awake again that night. "Well," Billy said, "there's needles and pins in it, and my lip's swollen isn't it? It feels like it's down on my chin."

We returned home and I told Pa that the dentist didn't have time to pull Billy's tooth, and besides Billy didn't have any ache now. The dentist had put some oil on his gums. If Billy cried that night, I was prepared to blanket his mouth so Pa wouldn't hear, but he must have gotten such a good dose of novocaine, the pain got scared and kept quiet. It wasn't until a week later that the tooth started up again. This time it was a jumping toothache, and Pa jumped Billy straight to the dentist himself. Either the dentist pulled it or Pa would pull it out with the forge tongs. So Billy ended up with a tooth in hand, a great place to have it.

No one could pry that tooth from his hand, because we had been led to believe that if it were lost before the tooth fairy took it – and it was picked up by a dog – you'd grow a dog tooth in its place, or any other animal's tooth for that matter, even if was a hen or a frog. Putting it under a pillow that two heads lay on, Billy dreamed about having no more toothache. We couldn't find the tooth in the morning – with all the shuffling and twisting of four heads on two pillows, we wondered how the tooth fairy had got at it, but she must have, as Billy didn't grow any animal teeth.

I'm Hooked on Cotton Batting

◦○◦○◦

During my school days, one of my pet peeves was cashmere stockings on girls. They didn't bother me on boys. But girls' irregular, vulcanized legs, bulging with long johns, were definitely sickening. My other peeve was cotton wool in someone's ears. And if a girl had a combination of the two, no matter how gorgeous she was, they could have sent her off to Alcatraz for all I cared and smothered her in wool and cashmere. I'd almost turn against Ma whenever I spied her wearing those long white cashmere stockings around the house. To me it was the same as scraping down a blackboard with your fingernails. Thank God she at least had good ears, with no cotton wool in them, or I might have gone completely berserk.

When I was seventeen, tourists from Georgia stopped near our house one day to ask directions to Indian Beach. The carload consisted of a mother, father, a brother and three sisters. Had they given me notice they were coming, I'd have changed my torn shirt and pants with the rearend out. Stuttering directions, I felt embarrassed, especially when I saw three young females in the back. It didn't take long for me to realize I was madly in love with the oldest one. She was the only one who smiled at me, and she was mine. What an angel. My heart missed a few beats. Oh, if only she could have said: "Andy I love you. Jump in the car, patches and all, and daddy will take care of you forever, as I know I've met my man." I was still in a romantic stupor as their car drove off.

I had to get to the beach right away so I could get this girl before someone else did. Galloping into the house, I tried for many minutes to make myself handsome. (A plastic surgeon might have helped.) I splashed cologne all over myself, frantically scrubbed my teeth, and combed my hair in all different directions. Then I gave that up and decided to tantalize my angel instead with my dashing clothes. I sped upstairs and tried on all my brothers' clothes. I then went on to Pa's cupboard, wanting to look as sexy as possible. (Pa always looked so sexy, when he was asleep.)

Presentable at last, (I looked like Charlie Chaplin without his cane) I ran down to the beach. Although there were hundreds of people on the beach, it didn't bother me a bit. Like Superman, my eyes homed right in on my sweetheart. Hustling into their bathing suits, the family was spreading out a large blanket. I hoped that it was for me and my love to lie on and plan our babies. Everyone was smiling, including my goddess, who had a mouthful of Ipana teeth which only added more fire to my yearnings. Suddenly, this girl I had fallen in love with through a car window was strolling toward me, like a mirage on the sand.

"Are you the one who gave us the directions?" I thought she might add, "I didn't recognize you without the rearend out of your pants," so I quickly replied "Yeah," with the authority of a tour guide (though in the state I was in, I could barely find my way home). "You're the people from Georgia." What I really wanted to do was get her alone and say, "I've loved you from the moment I first laid eyes on you, and now it's up to you to make the first move. Meanwhile, let's get rid of your family." Giving her a crooked smile (so as not to show her one of my front teeth which was a shade longer than the other), I told her my name was Andy.

Talking for quite a while on the warm sand, I was in ecstasy. All three sisters were there now, grinning and happy to know someone on the beach, even if he was named after a Panda bear. My beloved edged closer, with questions concerning the way of life on the island, and remarking on the beauty of the shores. Of course, I took credit for all of it, and was wondering how it would go over if I told them I had a hand in making the coal mines. After all, Pa'd worked there for years. I was at the point of claiming I had even discovered the province, along with Johnnie Cabot.

What a beauty she was! How could I bring myself to face Pa again when I went home? Quite a contrast between him and this lucious-faced girl. (Maybe I could get Pa to wear a mask.) Pointing across the harbour, I got my wests and easts well mixed, but she looked adoringly on me as if she presumed I was Dr. Livingstone. With the sisters on my left and her on my right, I was in the midst of instructing them as to where the largest coal mine was and how I got the diamonds out, when I turned quickly and looked right down into her ear at a piece of cotton batting. A tarantula couldn't have been worse. My breath stopped. My eyes burned. My legs weakened and my voice faltered. Cotton batting in her ears! I had to forcibly keep myself from saying, "Ugh, let me out of here." I wanted to holler as loud as I could, "Oh, Pa, I'm coming home!" All the loving thoughts I'd had for this beauty had smothered to death in cotton wool. My darling had gone to pieces and I'd sooner have kissed Mrs. Vint's cow.

Fumbling some excuse, back to the house I scooted, as though stung by a herd of bees, and giving her the impression I was a long distance runner who could only pause for minutes at a time. Yanking off the different bits of Pa's and Billy's clothing on the run, I thought no matter how hard Pa was to look at, at least he didn't have wool in his ears.

Many years later, I awoke one morning to find my ears in an uproar. Everything unbearable had made its home in my ears. Bells, horns, guns, kids crying, dogs barking, drills buzzing. The noise continued for days. But I couldn't be bothered seeing a doctor. He'd probably tell me I needed a hysterectomy. So after trying various home remedies, as the last resort, God help me, I tried cotton wool! Though the noise was still there, I couldn't hear it. The dreaded cotton had solved the problem.

Now I had a new problem, because I didn't want anyone to see my stuffed ears, not even my dog. Each day, when going to town, I would mash small mounds of cotton in as far as they would go. (I know one piece must have worked its way to the centre of my head, as I never did retrieve it. This probably accounts for the days I feel fuzzy headed.) To hide my puffy ears, I'd look people straight in the face when I spoke.

Another big problem was holding in the wool, that is keeping it in my ears. I'd pack it in as best I could, but when I pulled out my finger, I was also pulling the wool right back out on the snags of my fingers, like little Jack Horner and his plum. (Maybe plums would have stayed in my ears better.) I'd be talking to someone, pointing, gesturing, and to my amazement I'd hear pandemonium beginning again in my ears. Then I'd notice knobs of cotton on the ends of my fingers. It looked like I'd been making little finger puppets. The little white woolly wigs fit nicely right over my fingernails; and as I gestured with my hands, I was making them dance for people.

Another trial was losing my woolly bears completely. At a dance once, with a few drinks under my belt and a few pounds of cotton in my ears, I forgot about my ailments for a while. All I can remember of this evening is reaching out to the couple dancing in front of me and pinching my wool off a shoulder. I became an expert at this. It was a bit like swatting a mosquito, or catching a precious butterfly.

So you can see how my hatred of cotton-laden ears has backfired. I'm now hooked on ear wool and ear wool's hooked on me. I get giddy when I pull the absorbant wool out of a new bottle of vitamin E. I suppose that with my luck I'll soon be forced to wear cashmere stockings for my varicose veins.

Now if only those girls of yesteryear would come and ask me directions today, I would gladly stay with them – even if they had a bale of cotton in one ear and a sheep in the other. What's a little wool between friends? Why, we could sit on the big rocks at the bottom of the cliffs in Sydney Mines and swap yarns and wool. Who needs torpedoes, guns, elephants trumpeting, and cannons going off? There'd be enough of those going off after that big kiss. After which, we could just sit quietly, gaze out across the harbour, and smooth out our cashmere stockings.

PART TWO

•○•○•○•

WE CAN'T BLAME PA
FOR THIS

The Way I Am

°C°O°C°

If it seems that I've suddenly aged in the following stories, I have. And you can tell by these tales that I'm just as unglued as ever and that crazy things never stop happening to me. I'm still accident prone, but now when I fall down I don't get up as fast. And instead of Pa and my brothers worrying about me, my wife and daughter now pick me up. Over the years, like the old sea captains, I've travelled many places from Niagara Falls, New York, to Waltham, Massachusetts, and from Portsmouth, Virginia to Coburg, New Brunswick, where I make my home today, with my wife Rhoda and my Dummies (I'll tell you about them later).

As I said, I've been plagued by jinxes and insane happenings all my life. In the forties I lived for a while in New Brunswick. I was driving one of the first cars I had ever owned. Of course it was second hand, but it was better than pushing Pa's wheel barrow around, so I was quite content with it. One day I was travelling from my home in New Brunswick to Amherst, Nova Scotia. Coming to the turn-off in Aulac for Amherst, I grasped the wheel and turned to the left. Suddenly, as if in a nightmare, I was holding the steering wheel in my hand. It had broken right off the steering column! With traffic all around me, how was I going to steer the car, let alone save my life? Flinging the wheel on the seat beside me, I grabbed the shaft between my two hands as if I were a monkey climbing a pole. Twisting, turning and grappling with it as if I was struggling with a boa

97

constrictor, I finally wrestled the car over to the side of the road, and breathed a sigh of relief. I figured it would probably be safer if I got a good horse to get me the forty miles back and forth to Amherst. At least its head wouldn't come off in my hands.

My next crazy incident with a car came about four or five years ago when my family seemed to be having a real run of bad luck. My daughter's and her husband's motor had been stolen off their sailboat, someone had ripped down two or three flags that led in to my Dummy Farm, and a raccoon had cleaned out three rows of our ripened corn. I was dwelling on these unpleasant thoughts one drizzly night, as I made my way home from Amherst. Bumping over the railroad tracks, I knew I'd soon be turning into my yard for supper. All of a sudden – BOOM – a horrifying sound, accompanied by loud vibrations, shook the car.

This was it. I knew Edgar Hoover and his gang were out to get me this time and they meant business. Someone lurking in the bushes had shot at me. (Maybe it was Pa getting revenge for me breaking his teapot.) I was taking no chances with hidden marauders, so I ducked my head and slipped onto my knees on the floor of the car with my back brushing the seat, my eyes barely peering over the dash. (I now know how a midget would feel if he stood up on the floor of my car.) Swerving the car abruptly, I whipped into my driveway before they could start throwing grenades at me, pushing down hard on the gas pedal with my hand.

Then crunching to a halt, I tumbled out of the car and crawled to the door of my house on my stomach. Spilling my wild tale to my wife Rhoda, we rushed through the house closing the curtains and arming ourselves with brooms and mops. After a couple of hours of sitting in the middle of the floor, away from the window and holding our weapons, without any bombs being thrown or arrows shot through the kitchen door, I decided to go out and look around the car. With flashlight in hand, I surveyed it with a fine tooth comb looking for the bullet hole that must have made a hole the size of a pumpkin. Ducking, and throwing myself onto the ground every time a tree branch rustled in the wind, I found the car in perfect shape. There wasn't even a dent. Then I decided to check under the car, where I found a hole in the muffler the size of a grapefruit.

This was the second time I had narrowly escaped death at my car's hands. And it certainly would have been embarrassing for my grandsons to have to tell people that their grandfather had been shot to death by his own muffler.

Then there was the tussle I had with a grapefruit knife. A few years after I left Sydney, I met and married my wife, Rhoda, and we lived in New Brunswick for a while, just down the lane from her family.

One day, while she was up visiting her mother, I was going through the knife drawer, trying to find a sharp knife, when I came across one that was all crooked on the end. Plucking it from the drawer, I got the hammer and tried to straighten it out. That didn't work. I jumped up and down on the twisted end a few times, like a trampoline, but it bounced right back. I slapped it between two large rocks outdoors. Didn't do a thing to it. And when Rhoda finally made her appearance, she caught me sticking it in the crack of the door, and slamming the door on it. She explained to me that it was a grapefruit knife and that it was supposed to be shaped that way. What a relief! I was just about to take it to a blacksmith to have it melted flat in his forge. And if that didn't work, I was planning to drive to New York City with it and stick it under a cornerstone of the Empire State Building.

When I married Rhoda, I married into a hunting family. (The only thing I had ever hunted for was Billy, Murray, or Teedy when they were hiding from Pa.) One day, my wife's brother, Bob, and I drove back on an old logging road into the woods, his rifle standing on the floor between us, resting against the seat. Suddenly, Bob slammed on the brakes and jumped from the truck, shouting, "I see a pee vee." Calling after him, I kept repeating, "Here, take the gun. You forgot the gun." For a second Bob looked back at me, and smirked as if to say, "I can throttle this wild beast with my bare hands." I was thinking my heavens, these New Brunswickers are brave. This must be the sign of a true hunter: to be able to slay the animal without snare or rifle. But I wasn't going to take any chances, as I leapt from the truck, rifle at the ready. There might have been other vicious pee vees around, just waiting to jump out of the trees at you and dig their fangs into your shoulder blades.

In a few moments, Bob was walking in my direction carrying something that looked like a large hook, kind of like the one Captain Hook had after he lost his hand to the crocodile. Laughing, Bob told me that this was a peavey, a tool used for rolling logs. It didn't look too dangerous laying on the seat on the way home, but I kept a tight grip on the gun anyway, in case it decided to take a chunk out of my leg.

I've also had a lot of trouble whenever I'm in a hurry. I once rushed out of my house to make an appointment on time, when my raincoat got caught in the door as I closed it. I didn't notice it and I kept on going and ripped the coat right up the back. But that wasn't the worst of it. The door had a Yale lock which locked automatically as soon as the door closed; and the key to the lock was in my car, sitting way out in the driveway. Held fast by the door, I wracked my brain for minutes trying to figure how I was going to get out of this situation, until it finally dawned on me that all I had to do was take off my coat, and go get the key. Minutes before, I had had visions of freezing or starving to death, held up by nothing but a thin strip of cloth.

Another time, I was in a rush to get to town before the stores closed. I sped out to my car, took a quick look in the mirror to find my hair (what there is left of it) all askew, blowing in all directions, and very dry. I thought I'd just zip back into the house and rub a little Brylcreem through my hair to tame it. Running upstairs to the bathroom, I grabbed the little tube and squeezed out a goodly portion into the palm of my hand. Without even looking, I rubbed my hands together as if I was warming them over a fire, and massaged the cream all through my hair. I was wondering why my hair felt so stiff and sticky. Looking down at the tube, I saw to my horror, that I had covered my hair in toothpaste.

As you can see from the above, it never ends, which brings me to my Dummies. In 1967, during Canada's Centennial year, I figured I'd do something no one else had ever done. (I was also missing my brothers at this time.) So I thought I'd create a bunch of Dummies. They're mostly straw-stuffed mannekins, with javex-bottle heads and light–bulb noses, dressed in clothes I buy from the Sally Ann. I began with about twenty, but now hundreds are strewn across five acres of lawn and woods. Each one is equipped with a printed sign to describe his or her character.

For instance, there's a woman sprawled on a cane chair, hair in disarray, and a cigarette dangling from her lips. She sports the caption: "It was cigarettes that killed poor Aunt Rosy. Pa sent her to the store for some, but she was hit by the bus and killed, mind you."

In the eighteen years since the Dummies' beginnings, I've had dummy heart transplants here on my lawn, a dummy banana tree, a dummy still, and Christmas trees decorated year round. There are also Dummies in a small pond behind my house, fishing, swimming, and drowning.

Further along there's an old man stretched out on a cot. Two young women are sitting on each side of him. His epitaph reads, "Here lies Pa, he loved the women; he met the two, while he was swimming."

At one time or another, people from all over Canada, the States, and Europe have been in to see the Dummies. A small admission fee is charged, but there's a sign saying "If you don't laugh, you don't pay. We pay you."

The Dummies and I have travelled to the Burnaby Art Gallery in British Columbia, and they've been on television and radio and won many prizes at various parades. So drop in sometime. They're dying to see you and, who knows, you might even see yourself or your mother-in-law. And it won't cost a cent if you don't laugh, but if you do, you'll have to leave me everything in your will. And don't stay too long because we always have an empty chair or two, and the Dummies do have a way of taking over.

Quick, Give Me a Drink

◦◦◦◦◦

Many times in my life I got into trouble by just taking a drink, and I'm not talking about liquor. The first time was during a ball game when I was nine.

A couple of quarts of water on the baseball field didn't last long with twenty players rushing over for a sip all the time while the game was on. Now, there weren't many homes that would allow a ruffian bunch of players to march in all at once, surround the sink, and wait in line for a good swig of clear water. But there was one family, a family to out-do most families. They had two sons in the ball game, and they would greet any of us with the attitude that anything they had was ours.

This one hot summer's day the welcome mat was out as usual. The line-up of players was pushing and grabbing for one thirst-quenching cup. I was fifth in line. I wondered why they weren't taking this cup full of cool clear water sitting there on the side board. At the point where I could stand it no longer without water, I reached over six arms and clutched this untouched cup of water. I downed it with the force of a man in the Sahara Desert who had just come upon an oasis.

Just as I was being revived by the last drop of this oasis, the family's five-year-old kid went into a laughing fit and brought everyone's drinking to a halt. As I lowered the cup from my lips, the kid pointed at me and said in a giggly voice, "Ma's teeth in that cup."

It took some time for my brain to register what he was talking about. Then it filtered in. This was the cup his mother soaked her false teeth in. Why did he have to tell me? Didn't he know ignorance was bliss? But all ignorance and bliss were rapidly leaving my body, along with calmness and serenity. Had I left a few drops, I wouldn't have felt so badly, but I had drained every drop, including the sediments. Faster than I reached for the cup when it was full, the empty cup fell to the floor. I dashed madly through the screen door, almost taking it with me, amidst the screaming laughter of the whole baseball team. I'd like to have drowned that kid, (as well as his mother) in that horrible cup.

Whatever I'd eaten for the past year gushed into a watery ditch. I felt like getting a stick and feeling around inside to see if I could get up anything else that looked like it might have been in that cup. And to top it off, I had to go back to the game of laughing baseball players, still thirsty.

How happy I was, though, a few days later when I was talking to the kid's mother (with her not knowing I was detecting every move her mouth made) to find she still had her top and bottom sets in. This meant I wouldn't need an operation on my stomach to have her teeth pulled.

The next time I got into trouble drinking, it was the moon's fault.

All my life I'd seen Ma save small slivers of soap. Too small to wash your hands with, she would put the broken pieces in a container. These bits of soap were a great help on washday. The whole amount was thrown in with the dirty clothes, container and all, and there weren't any dirtier clothes than ours. For some reason I objected to this for as long as I can remember. I'd usually throw those small shavings into the garbage or burn them.

Thinking that no one but Ma saved these bits of soap, a few months of marriage and hand washing led me to find out that my wife was also a slick soap saver. Only Rhoda carried the soap shavings a bit further. She'd place the tidbits of soap in a glass, add a little water, and in no time they'd turn into a slime of softened soap.

Lifebuoy soap, with a deep orange colour and a strong smell, was used a lot during the war years. Then another soap glutted the market, a carbolic soap, much stronger and smellier than Lifebuoy. I did most of the shopping and this soap was my favourite and the cheapest.

We were living in Toronto at this time and my first job after landing there was a baker's route. I had a team of horses, a four-wheeled wagon with a canopy over my head to protect me from the elements and pigeon droppings. Two months after working for this bread company, I was invited to the baker's ball, which included a beautiful supper, drinks on the house and lots of bread. Not used to anything free, I didn't hesitate to accept the invitation, and I indulged a little more in the food and drink than if I had been paying for it. Weaving along the sidewalk on the way home, I seemed to have many legs.

When I arrived home at 2:00 a.m., Rhoda was asleep, but after dropping seven or eight shoes to the floor from crossed legs, she awakened. "That you Andy? Did you have a good time?" Now, no matter how drunk or sick I am, it always seems the good Lord gave me the strength to answer. Knowing I wouldn't be available for long conversations because I would probably die before sunrise, I muttered, "Pretty good, but I'm on my way out," as I hummed "I'm Headed For the Last Roundup."

After the roaring time I'd had at the baker's ball, all I wanted to do was lay down and fold my hands over my chest in preparation for my burial. I collapsed alongside Rhoda, went instantly asleep and knew no more. Two hours later a great thirst assailed me. I would have been happy standing underneath Niagara Falls for three hours with my mouth open.

I stumbled to my feet, not disturbing Rhoda's dreams, and looked in wonder at the beauty of the full moon shining through the kitchen window. I was definitely dying of thirst, but everything appeared heavenly in that light. Maybe I was already dead. I followed the path of the moonbeams. They came to rest on a sparkling glass of orange juice beside the sink. That's what my system needed. I don't remember us ever having orange juice in the house. The moon must have placed it there. What timing. I was in heaven. Humming "Jesus Wants Me for a Moonbeam," I tipped the glass way back, braced my feet, and the first two large glugs went straight to my stomach.

Rhoda was awakened by the gurglings of a man possessed by the full moon – who was quickly turning into a werewolf, a maniac, or both. I couldn't talk. I couldn't cough. I was strangling on the floor, a puddle of orange froth forming on my lips. Jesus might soon get me, but I wouldn't have made much of a moonbeam. About all I'd have been good for was the lion's roar at the end of the Metro-Goldwyn-Mayer movies. But I don't think it says in the Bible that there's much call for that in heaven.

I tried my best to convince Rhoda that I didn't have rabies, but that's hard to do, without words, while you're blowing bubbles. After my soap gargling, it was days before I could clear my throat or hum that hymn. My advice to any thirsty people out there is to never trust moonshine.

Another drinking disaster took place while I was working in Virginia, and it happened because I just couldn't keep my mouth shut, which is usually the case when you're drinking.

It was easier for me to eat my lunches at a restaurant, instead of going all the way back to my apartment. As a result, this waitress got to know what meals I preferred. It was a real help when she picked my meal, because I can only sit still a few minutes without telling some yarn. In this particular restaurant, coffee was available free after the first cup. Being a Scotsman, I was figuring I'd pitch a tent and stay the weekend.

Now, Southerners love to listen to the differences between living in Canada and the United States, and my audience was large this morning. Spicing my conversation with the goodness of Canadian living (mosquitoes the size of small potatoes), every ear was leaning into my story. Surrounded by diners, I was getting carried away. In fact, I was getting so carried away they should have had television cameras in there. I was definitely on a roll.

Rhubarb pie was the topic of conversation, and you know how exciting that can be. To my left was a sweet old lady who had never heard the word "rhubarb," let alone tasted the pie. She thought "rhubarb" was the name of a girl, and I must admit it does sound like some of those southern names like Magnolia and Butterbean.

I was letting my coffee cool to lukewarm, so I could enjoy the full flavour better. I noticed that the waitress had only filled this first cup half full. Oh well, I thought, I get all the rest free, why quibble over it. Then, to drive home my point about the ravishing rhubarb for the old lady's benefit on my left, I turned my stool toward her and spouted off in great detail.

Finishing my story, I spun my stool back into position to sip my coffee. If only I had sipped. What had happened was that while my back was turned, the waitress had poured me a boiling cup right off the grill. And I swigged so much of that hot liquid that had I been an elephant, I could have washed down the walls of the restaurant with the fiery fluid. I felt like spraying the waitress all over her face and hollering, "Great Lord, you've scalded me." I swished, rolled, tossed and shook that scalding coffee around my mouth. My listeners must have thought I was re-enacting a Canadian scene about how I'd once been attacked by a vicious man-eating rhubarb. The more I swished it around, the hotter it got. Even my fillings were steaming. Why couldn't someone have thrown a tray of ice cubes at my mouth?

None of the diners twigged to my predicament, even though my eyes were dripping with tears. They thought I had now become nostalgic about the death of a rhubarb and couldn't go on. My tongue had turned to leather. My teeth were screaming. It took every bit of ten scalding minutes for the hot coffee to cool in my mouth. I didn't dare swallow it. It would have burnt a hole through my belly button.

As a result of this episode, I don't ever want anyone to mention the name "rhubarb" to me again, even if it is the name of your girlfriend.

As you can see I do have a drinking problem. So as a result of all these happenings, I'm in no hurry for my drinks anymore. I sip very slowly. It's been a long time since I drank teeth, soap or caffeine volcanoes. However, I think I could still easily get a job as a sword swallower, a fire eater, or a box of soap suds. Now when I ask for tea, coffee, or soup, whether it's in a restaurant or at home, whoever passes me the hot liquid has to take the first sip. If smoke pours out their nostrils, they can keep it.

How Much Can You Take from a Ghost?

∘○∘○∘

Like Marley's Ghost, I think Pa was dead to begin with. Our family, scattered all over the States and Canada, all received telegrams to return to our old home in Sydney Mines, Nova Scotia for his funeral. Even though Pa had been terribly strict with us when we were growing up, he was a changed man once we were on our own and married. But we still called him "sir," even after he was dead.

Teedy got home first and came to meet me at the train station. I was relieved I wasn't the first to arrive, because I was still scared of Pa. I thought he might have answered my knock at the door. We made our way to our old house, and into the parlour where Pa's body was to be waked for three days. We doubted if Pa could wait that long; he was always a worker, and just couldn't keep still.

Mourners came by and we stayed up until 2:00 a.m., eating and talking about Pa with them. It was quite a dramatic scene with Pa laid out in the small front room. Here was the king himself listening to the whispered remarks of the visitors, as we sat in chairs around his coffin. One lady, sadly shaking her head, was saying, "My, he looks like himself." We could almost hear Pa's sarcastic reply to this: "Who did they expect me to look like, the undertaker?" An old bald-headed man from up the street was whispering to his friend, "He looks so well. Wasn't sick long, just a day. Someone should check around under his necktie. His heart probably never stopped beating. He's just lying there to see who his friends really are."

109

Just then a neighbour came in with her six-year-old boy, and although she was quiet and polite, the kid was yelping and jumping around. While his mother was viewing the remains, the kid had both doors open to the old book case (out of bounds to us for years) and was spewing papers all around. I looked over at Pa for help. Again I could hear Pa say: "Are you going to let it tear around like that, the little flamer?" I think Pa was about to reach out from the casket with his three-fingered hand and send the kid spinning with his stubs. We'd felt them ourselves a few years before.

Teedy said we wouldn't have to go to church anymore, unless we wanted to, and we wouldn't have to worry about finding someone to sign our report cards. And we wondered if we should put the key to Pa's trunk in with him (after we'd unlocked it first, of course). We were also discussing if we should send his knee boots along with him, but Teedy wanted to wear them at the funeral, if it rained.

Then, we took Prince, our seventeen-year-old dog, in to see Pa. We had taught him to sing years before by crying and howling different notes. He looked as if he was ready to break into "Abide With Me" without much coaxing.

Supper was soon being prepared and the smell of fish permeated the air. We almost asked Pa if he wanted a bite. He loved fish, and this was the first time it really sunk in that he was dead, as he didn't come out to join us.

After supper, we placed his pipe, tobacco and matches close by him on a table, in case he wanted a smoke when we all retired. That was the way we used to do it when Pa retired for the night. I told Teedy that when the undertaker pressed the lid down on Pa, he'd better be careful not to push too hard. Pa would probably push it right back up at him.

Now, Teedy was easily scared of ghosts (and so was I

for that matter), and what with Pa's wake and all, we began to remember all the spooky things that had happened in our house. The house had to be haunted. There were just too many unknown creaks in it. A few years before Pa's death, when most of us were still living at home, the house had been taken over by tennis balls. I remember Pa coming downstairs with a tennis ball in his hand, saying, "Who threw this?" only to go back upstairs to find three or four more bouncing around the hall. I saw many a ball bouncing in our house, but I never tried to pick one up because I had read many years before: "Never tinker with things that go bounce in the night."

Something definitely lived in our house besides us. I can vouch for that because things would always go missing. Once in a blue moon, in our teen years, we had steak for supper, in very small portions. I remember whenever my head was turned, I would go missing a piece of steak. Billy always said it was probably a ghost. But then I was sitting next to Billy at the table.

Anyway it was time for bed and Teedy and I were to sleep in the room next to Pa's bedroom. Ma had died twenty years before and now our stepmother, Blanche, and two young nephews slept in the next room in Pa's bed. It was amazing how some things never changed. Memories flooded over us, as Teedy took his position against the wall, while I settled myself on the side of the bed facing the window. Years slipped away as if in a time machine until we were about ten years old again. With my feet across Teedy's stomach, we drifted off to sleep.

About 3:00 a.m., when everything was quiet, Teedy roused me. "What's the matter? What do you want?" I said. Meanwhile, Teedy was sitting up straighter than Dracula in his casket. "Listen, what do you hear?" he whispered. I knew what he had heard, but pretended I was deaf. With a deadly grip on my arm, Teedy pointed toward the wall. "Listen, that's Pa's voice in there, groaning like he's in pain." I was fully conscious now and the groans were getting louder. I knew Pa's voice when I heard it. I'd taken orders from it for years and could even imitate it. But the main reason I let on I didn't hear the ghost was sheer terror. I didn't want to confirm Teedy's fears and have him dash out of the house to leave me alone to fight off Pa's ghost. One hysterical person in that room was enough. Better to wait it out until early daylight, then grab our pants and tear up to the Fire Station (where we could put our pants on). It was only a mile.

Now, whatever was in that wall was either fetched up on a spike or trying to tell us something in Gaelic. We figured we should put on the light, but we were ten feet from the switch, and as soon as we touched the floor, the ghosts would jump on our back (and some would probably take over our bed). Suddenly something cold and clammy touched me. The room lit up with a deep orange glow and the figure of a man stood in front of the bed. It pointed at us and said, "Oh, my heavens," then gave an agonizing moan. Teedy and I sat straight up and froze, sealed in body casts of plaster of Paris. Then the ghost took a full turn and we could hear it creak on the full fifteen steps down the stairs.

That was it. I wasn't going to wait for a second appearance. I pulled the sheets around me and started opening the window. In the darkness of our room, Teedy thought I was the ghost and took a swipe at me as he fell out of the bed, screeching for Blanche. I thought the ghost must have grabbed Teedy and I made a lunge at him, clutching the bedclothes all around me, looking like the shroud of Turin.

Then Blanche's muffled voice came back, "What do you want?" Teedy gave one screech and hollered, "Hurry up, for God's sake, get in here. The place is teeming with ghosts." In a few seconds, the door burst open and in rushed Blanche, plus the two nephews. They toppled right over Teedy and I in the darkness, knocking us backward across the haunted bed. Figuring that ghouls and poltergeists had now joined the ghosts, we got completely tangled up in our bedclothes. Suddenly the bed collapsed about our ears. The ghosts and demons really had us at their mercy now. Everybody in the room was now screeching. Blanche stepped into our pot and one of the nephews started bawling. Complete pandemonium reigned.

Finally, with the bed demolished on the floor, we scrambled to our feet, the other nephew got to the light switch and we began to calm down a little. We told Blanche she was going to have to stay with us on the floor, so we shoved her and the nephews in against the wall, next to the voice. If the ghost wanted someone, we would personally sacrifice the three of them to it, appease its spooky craving, and save our own skins. We weren't proud – not in front of ghosts anyway.

A minute later the groaning started up again, and Blanche said, "Well, that's Fred's voice all right." Teedy and I were a little braver now with our stepmother in bed with us, and we began to laugh hysterically when Teedy said, "How can that be Pa, Blanche? He's down in the parlour."

"You crazy buggers, go to sleep," mumbled Blanche, not too brave herself.

The moans continued all night, and here we were, two full-grown men, nearing thirty, sleeping with our stepmother and two nephews for protection, listening to Pa in the wall. When daylight finally came, we grabbed our clothes and, half-dressed, ran down the stairs to finish dressing in the kitchen – while Blanche was still sleeping with the ghost.

There was no way we were going through that again.

The next two nights we spent at a neighbour's and then we attended the funeral along with the rest of the family. But no money on earth would have lured us back up those stairs again, even in daylight with a posse. After all, five hours of intense groaning is about all a body can take, whether dead or alive.

Brother Bill, who had been in California and couldn't attend the funeral, came home seven months later and went upstairs to look around the old house, when he was almost knocked over by a pillow thrown at him. As Billy tells it, he made it down the fifteen steps in three giant leaps that he'll never forget and never try again.

And if you want to know what the groaning really was, you'll have a long wait. It was Pa and that's all there is to it. When you see Pa, you can ask him yourself, if he has stopped groaning by then. And he still rules us from beyond the grave. We got a collect call from him last Tuesday.

The Counterfeit Car Lot

❁❁❁

Years ago, we lived in Virginia and I was madly in love with convertibles, especially bright coloured ones. I'd picture myself parked, top down, a diamond-ringed finger hanging nonchalantly over the door, hair blowing in the wind, surveying the girls. My brother Teedy loved convertibles too. We'd hold our breath with an "Ah," whenever one slithered by. Why, I'd have been honoured to have been run over by one.

Convertibles were more expensive than hard tops, so we were on the look-out for a used one. Each night, we scanned newspapers and wrote down telephone numbers. We'd call people and get the same answer each time; that they'd sold the car the day before, even before it had appeared in the paper. But this hardly stopped our yearning. Teedy and I would take long drives in the country to surrounding towns (if our old car could take it), our eyes peeled for the no-tops. We'd come across a beautiful blue job on somebody's front lawn, slam on the brakes, and drive up the driveway praying for a miracle – like the owner saying, "Well fellows, I'm not so hot on convertibles. I'm moving to Tibet and I have no use for them. How about a trade? This gorgeous thing for your old pile of junk. I'll even throw in my house with the pool, if you'll just take it off my hands."

Used car lots closed on Saturdays at 5:00 p.m. This was our only day to hunt because we finished work at 4:00 p.m. We'd come upon some spiffy looking convertibles on

115

several used car lots, but the price the salesmen offered us on ours wasn't enough to buy a large bag of marbles. And no wonder; a fine wire was wrapped around the leg of the seat on the passenger's side to keep the door closed. Our old car was a gas guzzler, an oil burner, and she stalled a lot. It took her five minutes or more to stop, and she shook, rattled, and rolled. Salesmen just never took to our antique conveyance, and although I had new spark plugs, had changed its oil, it didn't do a thing to change the personality of our car. She was an old lemon.

With the price of two-year-old cars beyond our means, we now watched out for eight- or ten-year-olds. But these too were grabbed up by young men with the same fever, who lived closer to the lot, and who had far nicer cars than the one we were driving.

One Saturday we came across a huge car lot. This was the kind of car lot we dreamed about – four football fields long and hundreds of cars glistening in the sun. Both of us saw the car at the same time; a yellow and black roadster. We couldn't get out of our lizzy fast enough. Our dreams had been answered. Sprinting, leaping and dancing across the street, we were soon seated happily in the roadster's front seat, closing doors, feeling upholstery and dreaming. Oh my, this was our car; we'd have to have it at any cost! About ten years old, she was the answer to our prayers. There was no mistake about that. I opened the glove compartment. A shiny set of keys glistened at me! The salesman really wanted to sell this one. Teedy, in a trance, started the motor. And boy did she purr!

Wanting to know everything about this beauty, I grabbed the keys back while Teedy was still behind the wheel in a heavenly daze, opened my door, and went back to the trunk to do some exploring. This was just too good to be true, there had to be a hitch somewhere. The trunk held not only an unused tire and jack, but three full bags of groceries, with two cans of Canadian lobster in each bag. We'd trade in our old wreck for sure now, if for no other reason than to get that food. Had the salesman told us this roadster had a cracked block, a bad transmission, or even that there was a bomb planted in it somewhere, we'd snap it up no matter what he told us – even if I had to get a job moonlighting as a brain surgeon in Monte Carlo.

Back in the front seat again, I passed Teedy the keys, while I rifled through the papers and objects in the glove compartment. I switched on the map light, thinking this is the way I'd look to tourists while reading maps in Kentucky. Then, on the seat, I found another surprise. "Teedy," I said, "these kid gloves must have cost a pretty penny." I slipped them on. Perfect fit. I made a fist and viewed both my hands. Those kid gloves, nice and snug, gave me the feeling I could whip Joe Louis.

Suddenly, Teedy gave me a quick nudge. I straightened up. A heavy-set man with a long face was walking toward us. He was carrying some trousers and a coat on a hanger, covered neatly in plastic. Another prospective customer. He looked kind of disgusted; I guess because we'd seen this beauty first. Well, it was too bad for him. We weren't getting out. We'd outbuy him if we had to use force. Finders keepers. I was hoping he'd make himself scarce. Just keep going buddy.

Then Teedy figured out who he was. "Must be the salesman, just getting back from supper. But he's far from friendly looking." We understood, though. Who wants to work on a Saturday night? As the salesman drew closer, he glared at Teedy behind the wheel, then looked daggers at me sitting on the passenger's side smoothing out the tight kid gloves. We both gave him a big toothy grin, and I said with an affirmative nod, "We've found our car." As I patted the plush yellow upholstery, a look of proud ownership oozed from my every pore.

But my announcement didn't do much for the foul mood of the unsmiling man. He just bent over the side of *our* car and proceeded to hang his dry cleaning on a hook in the back seat, without even saying, "Excuse me." I whispered to Teedy, "We have a passenger already. Not only do we like the car, but total strangers want to drive in it with us." Then, old sourpuss stood up, faced us, and mumbled in every language but English. Seemed furious about something. Maybe something he ate. I thought salesmen always smiled. Must be ignorant. Fine way to sell cars. The car lot could at least have had a bilingual salesman. And what nerve! Hanging his clothes in *our* back seat. Obviously a poor upbringing. Pa could have taught him a thing or two.

Teedy tried again. "This is our car all right," he said, shaking his head from side to side merrily, and revving the motor. The man began pounding on the side of the car. So I asked the big question: "How much do you want for it?" We still couldn't follow his ranting and raving, and thought we should go to the sales office to find a translator. This guy didn't seem to know what we wanted. We kept trying to explain to him that *we* were going to buy *this* car. Maybe this was a new tactic salesman were using, kind of a reverse psychology.

He then went completely crazy, reached in and heaved Teedy out, while I scrambled out the passenger's side, still wearing the kid gloves. We raced away from the car, looking back over our shoulder in case he pulled a gun. We were going straight to the manager of the car lot to tell him his salesman wasn't fit to sell cars to Hitler.

As we loped over to the office, the man spun the roadster's wheels, gunned her out of the lot and sped off in *our* car! People like that should be locked away and guarded.

Trying to make excuses for him, we figured he must have gotten a cut in salary. That would make a person angry for sure. Walking toward what we thought was the car lot sales office, we came upon a large grocery store instead, and upon inquiring inside found out that we were in the midst of a giant shopping mall – and that the nearest car lot was three miles away!

Man, You're Burning Up

◦○◦○◦

In 1945, my wife, Rhoda, and daughter, Dianne, and I lived in Portsmouth, Virginia right across from the naval base in Norfolk. Every summer we'd head home to Canada to get out of the sweltering heat, so we could complain about the cold summers they had in New Brunswick.

Rhoda and I both drove, so it was a relief for me, after driving a long stretch, to sit beside her and relax a while. (But to be truthful, I have yet to relax while Rhoda is at the wheel. I wish they'd equip cars with two steering wheels, like airplanes, so I could take the extra wheel when Rhoda gets sleepy, instead of me doing her driving while she's still at the wheel. She tells me she's not sleepy, though I notice her eye closest to me is permanently closed.) Dianne, two years old, in the back seat piled high atop pillows, blankets, and food, would ask at least a hundred times, before we'd even left Virginia, "How long before we get to grammie's?"

Now, diesel trucks were new on the roads at this time. We knew nothing about them. Didn't even know what "diesel" meant. On this particular homeward journey, with thousands of cars on the Jersey Turnpike, Dianne was killing time by whining and counting how many trucks went past us, when suddenly she yelled, "Daddy, that truck is burning!" Before I could take this in, Rhoda started hollering. I thought she had fallen asleep at the wheel and was having a nightmare. She lurched ahead sputtering, "Andy, that

120

man's cab is on fire." I wrenched my eyes from Rhoda to the transport truck ahead of us. No doubt about it, the truck was just a rolling cloud of black smoke. I'd never seen anything like this in my life. Billowing black clouds all over. If the guy didn't pull over in a minute, he'd explode all over the highway.

The more smoke that escaped from his cab, the more concerned I became. Rolling down the highway, I poked my head from the window and yelled to the driver of the fourteen-wheeler, "Pull over, for God's sake, man. Your cab is on fire." He didn't seem to hear me. I felt like I should turn into one of those cowboys in the movies, jump from my car to the truck, pull the guy out of the truck, and jump to safety with him. But I didn't have my sneakers on.

Neck and neck now with the driver of the transport, I hollered and signalled to him again, with my head, neck and giblets dangling from the window. Frantically, I waved my arms in charade fashion, and hollered "BOOM" at him, trying to impress upon him that his rig was about to explode. "BOOM," I shouted again. He glanced over at me in a sad sort of way, as though I was a first class authentic nut.

For twenty miles, Rhoda didn't pay too much attention to the highway as, on my orders, she edged closer and closer to that big truck, like a spider creeping up on its prey. I now had fifty per cent of my body hanging out the right side of our car. I kept pointing at the trucker's cab and hollering, "BOOM, FIRE, VAROOM, KABOOM!" like Batman in the comic books. Then I began to think the guy might have a lot of troubles and want to go down with his ship. But I gave it another try.

"Closer!" I screamed at Rhoda. "Drive closer!"

"FIRE!" I yelled. "Don't be a fool, man! That's no way to go!" He still didn't seem to hear me – or want to. Rhoda

was now travelling about 75 mph to keep up with him and
I was now spilling 73 per cent of my body out the window,
like a rodeo star hanging over the side of his horse.

Finally, after about a half hour or more of this futile
life-saving venture, in which I had come pretty close to losing my own life and all the change out of my pockets, I said
to Rhoda, "Forget it, if the guy wants to burn to a crisp, he's
not going to take us with him." We had done all we could
for the guy with the death wish.

Trying to put the suicidal fool out of our minds as best
we could, we drove on for a few miles, when, across the
meridian, another transport appeared, passing us in the opposite direction. He was on fire too! As we continued on,
many diesel trucks passed us, all on fire! We began to figure something was fishy along with fiery. At the next gas
station, we inquired a bit about these burning trucks. The
gas station operator looked at us in amazement and asked
us where we had been for the last six months. He told us
that the new diesel truck's exhaust fumes went out through
the top of the cab. . . .

We didn't let on to a soul that we had stayed neck and
neck with one for almost an hour, and that I had come pretty
close to grabbing hold of the truck's handle and pulling it to
a dead stop with my brute strength.

Driving on a bit further, I began to get hungry, I guess
from all that shouting and leaning, so we pulled over into a
truck stop – and came face to face with our suicidal driver!

He looked at me kind of embarrassed, as if he was
scared of me. I felt like striding up to him and saying "You
fool. Did you know that I tried to save your life and that it
almost cost me mine?" Instead, I walked over to him, laughing good-naturedly, whacked him on the back, and said,
"Congratulations, you're the first person to see my new act.
I'm a clown for the rodeo."

T'Was Only a Pint

oOoOo

An elderly bachelor neighbour of mine called Trummy lived not far from me in New Brunswick. He was a real gentleman to meet. Living alone, he never bothered anyone, and was blessed with a terrific sense of humour, plus an old pair of rubber boots that were too small for me.

Enriched by Trummy's friendship and humour, I saw to it that I visited him almost daily, and had him over to supper frequently. And, in all modesty, the only thing he could do better than me was make home brew and chew tobacco. He must have told me the recipe for his home brew hundreds of times, but the times he gave me that recipe was always after I'd had a few drinks of it. After even one sip of Trummy's brew, I did well to remember where my lips were located.

Many times I visited him in the dead of winter, on the sly, with Rhoda thinking I had gone out to cut some wood. As the temperature dipped to the zero mark, he would point to the back of his oil range, the warmest part of his small house, where a twelve-gallon container stood smothered, choked, and strangled in coats. Eaton's and Simpson's combined didn't have as many coats as Trummy had over his beer. The brew, now in its second week of pregnancy, growled and snarled, bubbling with brown liquid, waiting for another two weeks before it went into labour, and was bottled and retired to the cellar.

Not wanting to miss the big event, I'd visit him almost

every night. On the fifteenth night, I had asked him: "What have you added to your brew?" to find out he had thrown in six ears of corn, a half dozen eggs, one turnip, bits of carrot, more yeast, plus six lords-a-leaping and a partridge in a pear tree. If I had taken over a burnt-out lightbulb, Trummy would have stuffed it into the concoction. (And that would have accounted for the agonizing groans underneath all those winter coats, as the broken lightbulb cut the six lords-a-leaping.) Nobody would have dared break into Trummy's house during this growling period. In fact, Scotland would never again have to use ganders to guard its vats of whiskey. All they'd need was one good batch of Trummy's brew in its second week, and anyone bent on stealing the whiskey would be deterred – thinking the vats were being guarded by hundreds of hounds.

I was over at his house one cold evening, and as usual Trummy was ever so glad to see me. "Come in Andy, and get warmed." I was having a beer this night and looking in the direction of the brew, when a heavy winter coat rose high into the air and fell right off the mixture onto the floor. The brew must have reached its kindling point. Trummy looked at me seriously and muttered, "That's all the yeast it can handle. Should be A 1 in a few days, if I can keep its wrap of coats on."

Beer Day finally arrived. Now, there were two routes to Trummy's, one along the main highway, where the police patrolled daily, and another along this dirt road. I took the dirt road. From my yard, I turned right, drove about one mile, then turned left, and about a block down was Trummy's. What a great memory I had for roads.

In a few minutes, I was driving up his lane. I backed my car around while it was still daylight, so I could make an easy escape later, while under the influence of Trummy and his fire-eating tonic. He met me with a broad smile, saying he'd just bottled his brew. "Good," I said, "now you can wear some of those coats you haven't had a chance to wear for a month." Two good-sized bottles were looking me right in the eye, along with some pints, and quarts, ready to be placed in his cellar. "Have one Andy, before I take them down. I believe this is stronger than the last batch." And with that, he placed a pint, still growling, on the table.

It was 8:00 p.m. and I advised Trummy that I'd have to be home by ten because I was expecting a long distance phone call. "Oh hell, you have plenty of time. Help your-self," he said quietly. Trying not to be too hoggish, I reached for the pint and pulled out the cork. It gave off some bright blue smoke, kind of like a scared skunk. Lifting the bottle to my lips, I took a good slug, and every tooth in my head stiffened.

"Wa-a-a," was all I could say. The roof of my mouth felt spongy and damp. On my second nip, I felt like I had been reincarnated. I just wasn't the same man who had arrived in my Jeep. I was a brand new man. I continued, between "wa-a-a's" to tell Trummy how much better this home brew was than his previous batch (all the while think-ing that I was eating a wonderful Chinese supper in Cairo). On my third sip, I asked Trummy for a colouring book and crayons, as well as the recipe. On the fourth shot, I made Trummy the sole beneficiary in my will and made him swear that he'd be in my yard next morning, early, to give me the list of ingredients to make my own beer.

If there was a fifth slug in that pint, I wasn't aware of it, because the hour for me to evacuate was approaching. Through the haze, I thanked Trummy, telling him over and over again not to forget about the recipe. Then I floated into my Jeep and turned in the direction of the road. It would only take me three minutes to get home. What a laugh! In my state, I could fly home faster than that. My Jeep kept trying to get the message through to me not to drive it, because I couldn't shift gears and it kept stalling on me. Now, I had only about two blocks to drive on that dirt road, until I got to my first and only right-hand turn toward home. I drove three miles and that right turn never turned up. Maybe they had closed the road off while I was at Trummy's. There was nothing to do but continue. I prayed to Allah for a miracle, still expecting that right turn to jump out at me. I was beginning to feel like old Henry Hudson searching for the North West passage.

At times the road narrowed, and I thought I was on a sidewalk. Driving further along, the road turned into two deep ruts. Hemmed in by trees, I knew I had to get my Jeep turned around and back out of this mess. I broke into a hymn, "Lord, I'm Coming Home, I Hope." I stopped and looked out at the jungle around me. Why, I could have been rafting down the Amazon. It seemed to be growing warmer, so I doffed a few clothes, thinking that the moon was the sun. Struggling for what seemed like weeks to get turned around, I remembered the axe I'd placed in the Jeep before leaving home. We never ever had a *sharp* axe (only when we killed roosters, and we had no roosters). Little did I know I'd be using a dull axe on a dead-end road, chopping out a place from the jungle to turn around in. But I cut away, never tiring, and started into my second hymn, "Have Thine Own Way, Lord." Finally, (and don't ever ask me how) I got turned around. I thought I'd relax a while before attempting the gruelling journey back through the wilds of Borneo.

Starting up again and floating forward, I noticed a clearing on the right. I figured I was somewhere around the wheatfields of Kansas by this time. I turned a flashlight on to see what time it was. I was flabbergasted to find it was 3:00 a.m., almost time to milk the cows, only I had no cows. Thank goodness for that. "Humph," I muttered, "I missed my long distance call."

After a few minutes, headlights were coming at me in the distance. I was saved at last! It was my wife's brother, Bob. Trummy was with him, laughing fit to kill. He even tried to coax me back to his house for another pint!

On the way home now, I developed a headsplitter, one of the worst ever known to man or beast, the type where they send Martians down to tap the sides of your head with small wooden hammers. My cap wouldn't even fit my throbbing skull. The next morning, after a fitful few hours of lying in a coma, I was embarrassed to look in the direction of my Jeep. It was covered with scratches, small dents, and mud. And its headlights peered at me as if to say, "You think you've got troubles? What do you think I've been through?"

I told Rhoda she'd better lay out our mourning clothes because we'd soon be attending Trummy's funeral – after I shot him and his recipe.

The Lady and the Turnip

◦○◦○◦

Ever since I fell off the grandstand, I've been hooked on smoking. More than a decade ago, I made a pact with a friend, Bob, to quit smoking. The first one caught cheating would be fined, and possibly killed by the other. My friend was a farmer, and I grew to hate him. He had plenty of work to keep him busy when the craving for a cigarette came on. He would rush out and bucksaw some wood, brush down a cow or two, or start painting the barn. I, on the other hand, was a Good Humour ice-cream man at this time – though without cigarettes, I wasn't in the best of humour. When the smoking urge seized me, there was nothing to do but grit my teeth and imagine myself with my hands around Bob's throat for having made the pact with me in the first place.

Every day, I drove in a circle a total of fifty miles along the coastline, my ice box loaded with hundreds of individually cut pieces of ice cream, packed in dry ice, and frozen hard as cement. Driving in my Jeep, I was always greeted by flocks of little children.

Now, the first day of our deal was quite a busy one for me. The temperature was in the eighties (mine was in the hundreds). It was a perfect day for selling ice cream; also for dying from lack of nicotine. On that hot morning, people could have been lining the roads for ice cream with their tongues hanging on the white line, but I had nothing on my mind but cigarettes. Earlier on, before I made my rounds, a fish peddler had entered the house and offered me a smoke. Politely, I told him I had just quit, while I bared my teeth and snapped at him like a mad dog. Showing him my steel will power, I lit his cigarette from my card of matches (and wanted to set fire to his hair). He had no idea I was thinking of yanking the cigarette from his mouth and smoking it myself. I fought off this urge and became absorbed in the process of eating my book of matches and nine of my fingernails. Finally, he left puffing merrily on his weed. I was left gnashing merrily on my teeth.

I readied my Jeep for the trip. Driving down the road, my obsession with nicotine increased. Up ahead, I spied a customer. A woman carrying a five-pound turnip (about the size of a cigarette I would have liked to smoke then) walked over to me. She said she had no money, but would I exchange an ice cream for the turnip. Turnip would taste good for supper, I thought, so I accepted the turnip, gave her an ice cream, and left.

The turnip sat beside me, quiet and round. Travelling a little further down the road, I was still in misery, longing for a smoke. Then I got so mad I slammed on the brakes. The turnip, as though alive, rolled across the seat and nudged my right leg. I tossed it onto the floor in a rage and started on my way again.

I neared the beach where many bathers, adults and children, would be waiting for the jolly ice cream man. A bottle of beer on this hot and humid day would be a relief for some of the adults. I wanted nothing in this world but a cigarette. But I was sure everyone on the beach and across North America knew I had quit, and I didn't want to let them down. Children with candy cigarettes dangling from their lips had been sent to torment me. Standing in my little Jeep, serving every outstretched hand, I began to go into another fit of nicotinization. At the stage where something had to be done quickly, and with business slackening some, I spied my turnip.

Sitting crossways on my seat, and with a few bathers standing around admiring my colourful wagon, I pounced on that turnip as if it were alive. People must have thought I was athletic and carried a football with me right in my truck to practise with. Growling, drooling and gnawing, I made my first big bite into the turnip. The crowd looked on in amazement, whispering that I must belong to the muskrat family. But I didn't care. I just bit deeper into that soothing vegetable.

Bob had probably been out separating milk while I was having this attack. I dreamt of separating Bob limb from limb and drowning him in his milk. I now drove on a ways to a smaller beach. Selling many bricks of cut-up ice cream, I knew if worst came to worst, I could always duck down on the floor with my turnip, taking wild nips like a cat with a small mouse. I was doing quite well now and my craving had calmed down since my bout with the turnip. Then, lo and behold, a truck pulled up next to me, with a large billboard on its side showing a picture of two sunbathers enjoying a Pall Mall. The more I looked at the truck, the worse I felt. Finally, I could stand it no longer. I wheeled my Jeep around and left the beach, the bathers, and the cigarette truck. I almost turned my Jeep over as I crashed into a small wooden glen that had no driveway. Out of the public eye, I lunged for my prey, and for five solid minutes I trimmed my turnip. All that was left was an odd peeling here and there.

With my turnip devoured, I had nothing to fall back on now, and I still had four hours of selling left. I had to get ready for my next bad spell. I needed help. So I drove for miles up an old washed-out, rutty dirt road to visit this old woman who was in her nineties. Everyday, morning or evening, she'd always be puffing on an old pipe. She was my only hope. I decided to tell her I wanted a cup of tea; then, when she went to get it, I'd sneak a puff off her pipe. I didn't like to push her at her age, but when she started in on a long story about her father and the Boer War, I felt like beaning her.

Scanning the room for the pipe, I couldn't even smell it. I asked her if she was still on the pipe. "No dear," she said, "I quit six months ago." I almost fainted dead away. With the condition my nerves were in, I got up, glared at her and, without touching my tea, stomped out the door. Lack of nicotine will bring the beast out in anyone, anywhere, even around ninety-year-old grannies. Why hadn't I picked up *two* turnips from that lady on the road, I thought, as I backed out of the old woman's yard. While driving home, I watched these farmers plowing and levelling their land, and thought I'm not going to bother another soul. I'll just buy me some rich land, plant acres and acres of turnips, and when harvesting time rolls around, I'll sit there twelve hours of the day and just gnaw, and gnaw, and gnaw. Because I wouldn't want to go back to that nasty habit of smoking. No way. But with my luck, after planting my turnips, just like Jack and the Beanstock, I'd probably grow a turnip stock that would soar to the heavens; and after climbing it, as I entered the giant's lair in the sky, he'd probably be sitting there in a haze, savagely puffing away, surrounded by cartons of cigarettes and pipes.

That Secret Operation

∘C∘C∘C∘

There's many a man my age who will have to have that secret rearend operation sooner or later, and I don't mean on his car.

Walking around straddle-legged for many days, avoiding sit-downs or sit-ups, my pains were all behind me. I can't stand hospitals, so I tried hard to avoid the place, until I was absolutely forced to see an M.D. My case was diagnosed as strangulated hemorrhoids. They were going to choke me from the bottom up, I thought.

My symptoms were large bubbles on my hind parts – which couldn't be touched with a feather, fanned, or even breathed on (as if anyone would want to get close enough to my bottom to breath on it). I couldn't even stand anyone using my rear as a point of reference. Sitting down was a thing of the past. Standing up was impossible because the blood rushed to my bubbles and they felt like they were about to burst. About the only way to get through life from here on in would have been as a ghost. A sturdy coat hanger might have been the answer, if I could have flung myself over it belly folded in. I couldn't lie down, and I could only walk like a penguin at a snail's pace. The whole mess was so painful, I was capable of murder.

Now, there was really no remedy for this illness, other than being in a drunken state lasting throughout eternity. (It should be listed with such mortal wounds as shark attacks and bull gorings.) But in the country, every farmer and his little daughter have cures for every ailment the body gets, up to and including leprosy. I was willing to try anything. Weeks went by and I treated myself with remedies muttered by old Aunt Lucy or Uncle Ned. Heat was what it needed, lots of good old heat, they blatted. Why, I would have sat on our wood stove for an hour if I could have balanced just right with someone holding each of my arms. A heating pad would do the trick. Except that all it did was fill my bubbles full of hot air. If I'd kept it up, I'd have been floating through the air like a weather balloon, bottom side up.

Further recipes included woollen underwear with a dash of vinegar, a loose skirt (be you male or female to keep the tightness from the sore spots), and last but not least, a goose feather pillow tied to your rearend. Then you had to stand erect for the rest of your existence. Everybody who saw me in this condition was affected by it and walked away lame – after I had told them from what I was suffering.

Finally, tired of my pain, Rhoda said one day out of the blue sky that she was calling the hospital. What sheer craziness! What on earth for? Just because I was walking around like a man of 185? I despised hospitals, the antiseptic smell, the bed pans clanking against each other, and the way they put people to bed early like Pa used to do to us.

"Bring him in immediately," said the doctor. The shock was so great, I put up no resistance. I was too sore to change from my pyjamas, so I donned a top coat and we were off to camp. Not an inch of my rear touched the back seat of the car, but I was balanced: clutching the back of the front seat, hawk-like, I hovered in mid-air like a helicopter the twenty miles to the hospital, gritting my teeth all the way. (After this, I'd need a trip to the dentist.)

An Irish doctor examined me on arrival and, with a

sigh, as if to say, "I'm surprised this man is still alive, the condition his bottom is in," hustled me off to bed and ordered my bubbles to be encased in ice cubes. I thought of old Aunt Lucy and her heat prescription. I was ready to knead melted gum into her hair. But my the ice felt good. I had no more pain and I was able to lay out straight, without curling up like a worm. I could have relaxed there forever, unless there had been an ice shortage. Then it would have been off to Antarctica for me to straddle an igloo. Had I known intense cold was required, it would have been so easy for Rhoda to empty the deep freeze some and plop me astride the frozen vegetables, with the cover up so I wouldn't be asphyxiated.

Then the doctor informed me the operation would be done when the swelling was reduced. What operation? I was under the impression they'd just keep me in bed packed in ice – forever, if necessary. Then when I died, I'd be all ready for suspended animation; they could lock me away in an ice chest until they found a cure for what I had died of (freezing to death while being treated for bubble bum).

Next morning, I was wheeled down the corridor to the operating room, under the influence of a needle that was just starting to take hold. I was forcing myself to stay awake, so I could tell them how to perform the operation. A masked nurse came toward me. I couldn't run as I was strapped in bed. I hid my eyes like an ostrich, so she couldn't see me. I stopped breathing, so she wouldn't know I was alive. I prayed they wouldn't give me a heart transplant by mistake. What I needed was a complete rearend transplant.

The operating room was loaded with masked gunmen. Even my doctor had a bandana over his face. They didn't want me to be able to identify the ones about to butcher me. For some reason, the doctor asked me a few questions about women. Who did he think I was, a gynaecologist?

Who cared about women at a time like this? Right then, I wouldn't have cared if every woman in North America was on a raft headed for Africa. I felt we should have been talking about things like God and heaven, and about how my barber was ever going to be able to sit me in his chair to give me a haircut again. (He'd have to suspend me on a piece of nylon thread over his chair.) Then another crook popped up behind my head. He was the one who put me to sleep without a punch. And that was it. From there back to my hospital room bed was a blank. (I was dropped into my nest. The bandits walk away pushing their empty wagon and rubbing their hands and snickering. Days, months, years slipped quietly by in a few hours.)

When I woke up, my roommate was firing off a few funny lines at me about the operation. Unravelling my thoughts, I asked him if my baby had been born yet, and if not, when they were going to take me down to deliver. Good news: I'd been there and back, and I was still alive. Now maybe I'd be ready for the land of *Little Women*. I opened my tired eyes. It was real hard to figure out what part hurt.

All at once, I sat up and had the feeling that I had been cut in two like a beef. Bravely, I watched the small wheels on a nurse's wagon roll into my room, not dreaming they'd come to a halt at my bed. If anything, they should have brought in all the nurses and doctors with large oriental fans to cool off my rear, while I sang, "You made me what I am today." I wanted no one to see me, not even my wife. They'd ruined my behind. It still hurt when I yawned or blinked.

The doctor had a rubber glove on his hand and I figured he must have just come from doing the dishes. He smiled and said, "Andy, now this won't hurt," as he told me to lie on my side. What he did next should have been reported, and he should have served a prison term for it.

When I peered over the sheets, I saw the nurse was still there, and had placed a screen around me. Well, that was better. They must have been trying to make it nice and quiet for me. She then came toward me with a long-tailed can. "It's your enema," she purred happily, while fitting her hands into a set of powdery gloves. My enema? I'd never met an enema in my life. I figured it must be a wild animal from Malaya that pounced on people who had had recent operations.

The evil enema enemy soon had me pumped so full of bubble bath that it could have filled a swimming pool. The nurse asked me if I thought I could go to the bathroom by myself. "Well, of course I can. I was toilet trained by the time I was old enough to drive a car." Besides I didn't want a whole army coming with me on this critical mission.

The main lavatory was at the very end of the hospital hall. But there was a tiny four-foot-by-four-foot toilet at my end; I'd go to it. Lawrence Welk's bubbles were really working now. Churning and bubbling like a volcano that was ready to erupt, the loveliest feeling in the world washed over me as I reached for the doorknob to the little toilet. It felt as though I was drowning and someone had just thrown me an inner tube to save my life. All control switches holding back my oceans of water were chugging, straining, warning me, and slowing me down considerably . . . I eased open the door extra gently, with a relieved smile on my face. My whole outlook was changing. I would soon be a new man.

Suddenly, a loud female screech met my ears. I think one came out of me too. All my engines went into reverse as the noisy commotion brought the young nurse into the toilet with us, probably expecting a rapist. "See here," I said, "why is this lady on my seat? Toss her out, Nurse, this instant. I have to sit here, quick, before it's too late – for all of us."

The nurse held back a laugh. I, on the other hand, could hardly hold anything back. I was drowning again in my own bubbles; every muscle in my body was on "hold it," knowing I'd have to head for the far toilet in my lowest gear. Like a drunken kangaroo, I did my best, inching my way. Ten feet or more, I thought, and I'd have it whipped. Praying that no one got there before I did, without warning I was attacked by a wheel chair. Who'd ever have thought there would be a four-wheel vehicle on my flight path? It was propelled along by an arthritic old man who did every twist imaginable to avoid hitting me. I felt like jumping on his lap so he could speed me along to the john. He kept smiling and pardoning himself in a friendly way, but I couldn't even show my forgiveness with a hand signal. Too risky. Might start leaking. A slight wink showed him I accepted his apology, while I skimmed along at the point of no return, about to explode.

I reached for the closed door, turned the doorknob, and walked right into the storage room! Mumbling in Greek, out I went again, figuring I should have grabbed a wheel chair for myself, preferably one with a large pot under the seat. I trundled on gamely. Just a few more steps. Another door. Pushing it open, I came face to face with the Hospital Administrator! I had entered his office. Almost choking with rage and bubbles, I spewed out, "Where in Hell is the toilet?" Pointed in the right direction, I waddled off like a large sea animal. Finally I made it to the right boiler room and luckily no one was there. A new world opened up, and I was saved by the plunger. Mission completed, I then took a bath, lurched my way back to my room, eased my rear into bed, and was soon dreaming of joining all those females on the raft to Africa.

Eventually, I healed up completely. As I think back, I have a few suggestions for hospital users: wheel chairs should be equipped with flashing red lights and patients having the same operation as I did should be issued a tomato can on arrival, wired around their waist so that it hangs just below their critical parts. And before the gruesome trip to the hospital, make sure your suitcase is well stocked with hand grenades, so that any doctor or nurse coming in your direction with gloves on or carrying a long-tailed pan, can be picked off in seconds.

From Rags to Riches to Rags

◦C◦C◦C◦

My most unforgettable moment ever had to be the night of the Olympic Lottery draw, September 28, 1975. That night I won fifty thousand dollars, and lost it again within the space of fifteen minutes.

I had often wondered what I would do if I came into a fair amount of money: buy a silver toupee, get my teeth capped with diamonds, invest in a herd of Brahma bulls, pick up some gold shingles for my barn, buy one of the Egyptian pyramids (or maybe two), and perhaps take a trip to the moon on gossamer wings. For this particular draw, I had bought three tickets for me and my wife. As well, my brother-in-law had talked me into going halves on a ticket with him. So I had him sign his name on the one shared between us, to make it legal.

Now, my red-headed, husky nephew, Pat, then eighteen, had recently moved from Ontario and spent most of his time with us. With the gambling instinct of his uncle embedded in him, he was with me the night of the draw. Strong-willed and stubborn, he persuaded me an hour before the program to let him have my brother-in-law's ticket to monitor, as I had three of my own to take care of. He told me over and over again before the draw that he knew what he was doing, because his brother had fifteen tickets on the last draw, and he'd checked them for him. This was good enough for me.

Picture the scene: the nervous hour was approaching

fast. An order came from Pat, "Don't speak to me." I could see by the glaze of concentration settling over his eyes that he didn't want to be bothered in any way. He straightened out the ticket and got his paper and pen ready to jot the numbers down.

The first number appeared on the screen. Pat set the ticket aside and wrote down the first winning number. The MC repeated this number several times. I was ten feet from Pat, closely checking the numbers on the tickets I was holding. Convinced that I had got nothing on that number, I turned to see my nephew's eyes watering. It even looked as if his head had shrunk. Suddenly, he went into a screaming fit, yelling, "Ya won!" The number of times he said "Ya won" in a second was unbelievable. "The very first number! Ya won, ya won!" he screamed. Trying to quiet him down was hard as I was now out of my mind myself. I crumpled up my tickets, thinking to hell with them, all I care about is the winning one Pat has. I even turned the television off after that first glorious number, harbouring a fleeting greedy thought as to what ever possessed me to go halves on that one ticket with my brother-in-law.

At this point Pat was red from stem to stern and I couldn't control his antics. "My God," he chortled, "you guys got fifty thousand dollars on the very first number!" He tore at the heavy woollen shirt that was beginning to suffocate him. I was about to rip a few clothes off myself, but thought better of it – I wanted to stick close to my ticket and Pat, in case he absconded with it. But I did kick over a chair or two and flung my cup of tea against the wall like they do in Russia.

Walking was suddenly much easier I found. There seemed to be no weight on my legs at all. I developed tendencies to leap and fly with no trouble. I had never known that a man in his late fifties could jump four feet off the floor. That was nothing for me. I seemed to have wire springs under my feet and felt that if I kept jumping up and down, as though on a trampoline, I could have leapt right through the roof, into the atmosphere. I could have flown over to pick up my winnings, or bounced there like a kangaroo. When I spoke, my top lip stayed up on my gums. When Pat talked to me, my ears closed up like they were plugged with mashed potatoes. I couldn't speak without stuttering and I ended my sentences before I was finished. I ran forward many times to look in the mirror, not to see if it was me, but to see what I looked like now that I was rich!

Even the old cat seemed sweet, young and wanted by me; and I was never overly fond of cats. Impulsively, I grabbed Tammy and kissed it directly on the mouth. The cat had an inkling something spectacular had happened. Here it was after 10:00 p.m. and I was singing, dancing and dishing out some leftover hamburger for its second supper of the evening. I even passed it a napkin. I looked at our furniture in distaste; and while I was in the process of throwing the old chairs out the door, all I could see were dollar signs.

My wife, Rhoda, was up the lane, mothersitting. She was also watching the draw. This was too much joy for me alone. I couldn't dial fast enough and wished I could have given one good, lung-splitting screech to bring her to the phone. She had quit smoking three weeks before. As I was telling her the great news, her heart started pounding so violently, she grabbed one of her sister's cigarettes to see if it would calm her down.

Not realizing she was almost having a coronary herself, she said to me, "Okay dear, now don't get excited. You might have a heart attack." Hearing her call me "dear" was more of a shock than winning the money. I hadn't heard that word from her since the minister paid us a visit.

With light, tingling fingers, I hung up the phone, but just for a few seconds. I called my wife right back to verify if the number that Pat had written down was the winning number. Perfect. Perfect. Every digit was right. Again, I heard from my wife, "Hang up, dear, you're getting too excited." She said this in a very sweet voice as though we'd always been the best of friends. For a minute, I thought maybe I should pack my bags and run away with all that money. But I couldn't be too greedy. I hung up again for a few more seconds. Who else could I share this wonderful news with?

Ah, my daughter, Dianne. I spewed out the news to her and her husband. They were flabbergasted, ecstatic and worried about how they were going to keep it a secret. By this time, we'd decided not to tell anyone outside the immediate family, for fear of kidnapping. Dianne rushed upstairs to her oldest boy's bedroom. She told David that his grandfather had just won fifty thousand dollars (by this time we'd taken possession of my brother-in-law's half) and whatever he did, not to tell a soul at school next day. She was ready to awaken Michael, age seven, something she'd never normally do (as it was such a relief to have him asleep at last).

Meanwhile, back at my house, Pat continued to throw his hands to and fro, and wouldn't allow me to touch his writing pad or the ticket. He was still repeating, "Look what ya won! My God, look what ya won!" Though it was past 10:00 p.m., I was just about to take every family with a light on out for Chinese food. To hell with the expense. It couldn't be over fifty thousand dollars.

Pat reached to the end of the table for the winning ticket saying, "We'd better take good care of this, we don't want to lose it." Quietness reigned for seconds after this, and a different colour – green – engulfed his head, as he gazed upon the ticket.

"My God, what have I done? Damn it, damn it!" echoed through the house. I knew I was falling from a colonel to a buck private fast. "What? What?" I screeched, not wanting to hear the answer. Pat was looking from the ticket to the winning number he had put down on the writing pad. What had happened to my winning ticket? With paper in one hand and my ticket in the other, Pat made signals for me to shut up so he could tell me about his horrible mistake. Slowly, sadly, the story tumbled out. I was ready to shed my skin and eat it like a frog.

When the first winning number had appeared on the television, Pat had immediately written it down. At the same time, he had pushed the ticket out of the way, so he would have room to write the numbers down. His straining eyes focused only on the number he had written on the note pad. And when the MC repeated this number, Pat had followed each digit closely from the pad. Then swelling, steaming and bursting at every number, he knew that before him was the winning number. (And why shouldn't it be? He had just copied it directly from the television screen!) The about-face came when Pat compared his ticket to the number he had written down and found to his horror that the numbers differed like night and day. After I went over the number on the ticket myself, I found it wasn't even close to the winning number, from any angle. Not a digit matched. I was completely mortified. Sick wailing moans (Pat's and mine) filled the room – like people being mangled in a sausage machine.

Eventually, I came to my senses enough to know that I had to break the sorrowful news to my daughter and mothersitting wife, which would bring our fifteen minutes of wild living to an abrupt halt. My dialling finger weighed a ton. I wished I had had to dial one hundred numbers before reaching them and then be blessed with an attack of laryngitis. When Dianne answered, before I had a chance to say anything, she told me I had interrupted her thoughts as she'd been making plans for a trip abroad for her and her husband, paid for of course by my winning ticket. In the background I could hear David hollering, "Grampy will probably buy me twenty new stamp books."

I hung up after giving her the bad news and slowly dialled my wife. When I told her, she seemed to take it rather well, a little too well. After that, I couldn't think of enough names to call Pat for his blundering. I told him bamboo shoots stuck through his gums wouldn't be punishment enough. If he'd had any money at all, he said he would have gladly given me every penny. And I would have taken it.

Now, the more we talked over what had happened, the funnier it became. Soon we were going into fits of sick laughter over Rhoda and I having coronaries over nothing, and my brother-in-law, who would never know how rich he almost was. More hysterical laughter rang out when we began to realize that if Pat had continued to copy down each of the remaining winning numbers, in the same manner as he had done with the first one, I'd have walked off with all ten prizes. Quite a feat since we only had four tickets.

Soon, my wife flew through the front door, a worried look on her face. She had rushed down from her mother's to see if I was serious about not winning the money. She thought I had told her I hadn't won to hide the fact that I really had won from others on the party line, who might have been listening to my first winning phone calls.

When the reality that we hadn't won a cent finally sunk in, she sure didn't call Pat or me dear any more. But, after a few moments, she began to laugh as hard as us. That night we laughed on and off until two in the morning, realizing that we were probably the first people in the world to experience the feeling of winning fifty thousand dollars without actually winning it.

There was another draw coming up in a few months. If I bought a ticket, it would be in secret. There would be no more nephew in my presence when that draw took place. I'd have him locked up for that night, or maybe for that year. I'd even try to be good to the old cat all through the night, and not pull the same stunt I had after learning of Pat's mistake.

Realizing I was just as poor as I had been before that brief fifteen-minute interlude, I now looked sharply at the cat and said, "Well, old boy, you've had your loving for this night." There were tears in the old cat's eyes as its schizophrenic bewhiskered master picked him up, opened the door, and threw him out into the cold fall night.

The Egg and I

◦◦◦◦◦

Looking beautiful isn't easy. All I see all day long is my wife, Rhoda, wandering around the kitchen, tapping her chin with an open hand. That, she tells me, prevents a double chin. But I say a double chin, or even a triple chin, is good in some ways. An extra chin or two will hide that crepe neck.

How many of you, after reaching middle age, instead of saying "Mirror, mirror on the wall, who's the fairest of them all?", say "Oh no!" to a new wrinkle on your face, next to the five thousand others? I say blame it on television. It's doing its best to keep us young, no matter how hard we fight against it. Television and youth have possessed Rhoda's brain. For almost a whole year, she had me doing yoga. It was a big strain for me, but she insisted I looked better, and even walked better. I don't know if it was flattery or not, but I fell for it. However, a while ago, while in the midst of a headstand, instead of staying in the vertical position, I continued right on into the fireplace, and was in a cast for weeks.

Rhoda has gone food crazy, too. If she caught me eating a slice of white bread, she'd probably call the police. Whole wheat, yes, but no fried eggs (they cause ulcers); just boiled ones without the yolk. I have ten laying hens and have yet to come across an egg minus the yolk. And I must not touch one strand of bacon. It's been smoked and filled with nitrates, which have been found to cause more damage than asbestos to the body of a rat – but I'm not a rat, yet. And touch not thy salt. Imagine trying to eat the white of an egg without salt. All canned soups are out of bounds too – she saw it on television – because monosodium glutamate causes brain damage. We are only supposed to use gauze tea bags – the paper ones are poison. Don't ask me why. It said so on television. However, the paper tea bags do have a creosote taste, and creosote is used to preserve railroad ties. So all I can figure out is that if you continue to use the paper ones, you're just asking to get hit by a train.

Rhoda will let me eat all the raw food I want: carrots, turnips, pumpkin, onions, garlic, lettuce, green peppers, radish and apple trees. But I don't want any. I'm too busy and haven't got the time needed to chew them up. Now you take bread or eggs. You can take a chance and swallow them without even chewing, but try swallowing a raw carrot, a small squash, a stock of celery, or the limb of an apple tree without chewing, and you'd better have some soul handy who has studied the Heinrich maneuver for choking.

We're the only house around that has vitamins after E. I believe my wife actually makes them. She tells me never to go without my vitamins. The days when I do, she says she gets a froggy feeling when she touches me in the morning (and if I continue to go without them, my skin will peel right off). Our shelves are lined with bottles lettered from A to Z. Anyone coming to our house would think we were running a nursery school. Often Rhoda will encourage me to take a half a bottle of vitamin C at one sitting – and that's okay if you don't mind spending your entire life on the toilet.

If I happen to eat more than usual, my wife knows just what vitamin caused it. She heard it on the telly. A few weeks ago, I had a ringing in my ear, so she gave me vitamin R for ringing. Every once in a while, loaded with vitamins and feeling like Tarzan of the Apes, (after just having told me never to miss my vitamins), Rhoda will skip one or two days – and not give me any. During these times, I get weak. I'm not as frisky as before. In a daze, I can't remember the day, and my speech changes. While sitting, both my arms seem to lock into a folding position, and I look as though I'm resting, but I'm not. Now, I'd say that's a good way to get rid of a person. Keep them hooked on lots of vitamins for weeks and weeks, then suddenly halt everything. I know, I developed everything from headaches to dysentry, and finally yodelling. It's when I get to the screeching stage that Rhoda puts the vitamins to me fast.

Rhoda next had me on yogurt for months. I thought I had a good excuse for refusing it. I told her it gave me cramps. She said it was supposed to give me cramps. Next it was brewer's yeast. It nauseated me and gave me liver spots. But Rhoda said being nauseated was good for me. It meant my body toxins were moving. As for the liver spots, she said they were an improvement, as they gave some colour to my wrinkled hands. Lately, she has learned that all packaged cereal is terrible for a person, especially me. So instead of asking me at breakfast if I want any shredded wheat, she's just stopped giving it to me. Red River cereal was next. For a whole week, every bowl and saucer in the house was running over with the stuff. Eating this cereal, we didn't need any bran. There was enough roughage in that box of cereal (especially combined with the half bottle of vitamin C), to keep you locked in your bathroom with a stack of magazines for weeks.

I'm not supposed to drink water while I'm eating. It does something to my saliva. Thins it out and floods my digestive system. And I'm not to drink before or after eating. Interferes with my hyperacidity. So now I can't drink water at all, because I'm either just getting ready to eat or just finishing up. Meanwhile, I'm turning into a tumbleweed.

I am allowed to eat all the wild onions, dandelion greens, and alfalfa sprouts I want. I really think Rhoda should have put me out to pasture in 1980. As it was, I did take nibbles of all this stuff, and felt much the same as before, except for the tendency I now have to paw the ground with my forefeet, toss my head from side to side and bellow like a caribou during the mating season.

I was much healthier and happier in the days before television or radio (and younger too). I never knew a thing about the good or the bad of this or that (except for the girls we ran around with). In my day, whatever was placed on the table, even if it was a fricasseed hedgehog, everyone ate it – without a thought in the world as to whether it was bad for you or not. The only thing we worried about was whether there'd be enough hedgehog to go around.

I remember salt herring sometimes gave people a touch of heartburn, but a spoonful of soda (four cents a pkg.) would counteract the acid from the fish, after a good solid burp. Today, television will even come up with a new name for heartburn (possibly Padunka) and a costly remedy to cure it – probably rare almonds from Morocco.

I've been to doctors off and on for the past few years, for check-ups and such, and I try to follow their suggestions for easing tension and stress. Not too often, but once in a while when I'm not feeling up to par, and I'm grouchy and nervous, I'll take a valium and relax for a while. This happened just the other day. Rhoda knew I was tired and jittery, so she gave me one of those little pills and left me to relax and unwind in my writing room.

I had just entered a stage of deep relaxation, an almost trancelike meditation, when the door to my room opened. Glancing up, I saw Rhoda with her mouth tightly closed. Making guttural noises, she kept pointing at her face. Why didn't she say something? Tight, drawn and motionless, her face was very different from when I'd seen her half an hour before.

"My God!" I thought, "She's having a stroke!" Not saying a word, she kept pointing to her face. I noticed part of her neck was pulled up. This didn't help calm my nerves. I spoke up loudly, in case the stroke had deafened her as well. "Why can't you talk? Are you having a stroke?" All she did was wag her head listlessly in a negative manner. Maybe it had affected her brain. Whatever her illness was, it was bad, because her speech had completely left her. At any moment she might collapse onto the floor. I wondered if I should take three more pills to get me through this.

All of a sudden, she waved her hand in a "wait a minute" way, and left the room. She seemed to be walking normally. Then she came back, still speechless. (Maybe her tongue had worn through from eating all those vitamins.) In her hand she carried a pencil and pad. In what looked like a very weak script she scribbled, "I had a facial, and my face is all puckered up." Then she scribbled some more: "Will you take one?"

Still coming out of my trance and in a state of shock, I didn't even know what the word "facial" meant. I just saw the words, "face is all puckered up." By the time I had followed her scrawl to "Will you take. . . ?" I automatically thought the rest of the sentence would be ". . . me to the hospital."

I spoke again, this time very weakly, "Are you taking a stroke?" No, no, she wagged, still not talking, with her motionless face. Again, she wrote on her pad, "Why not have a facial?" By this time, the message was getting through to me. She was not having a stroke. But she'd almost caused me to have one. She had just had a facial. My blood curdled. I yelled from my calm, restive position: "Why in Hell would I want a facial? I believe you're going crazy!"

She left the room, but was soon back with a saucer and a concoction of egg whites and honey – which was supposed to tighten the face and lessen the wrinkles. I was fit to be tied. On reflection though, I thought the facial just might help. But I don't think there's a recipe that tells you how to rub honey through a beard.

Anyway, I'm not going to try to look young anymore. I haven't got the strength for it. I'll just listen to that quiet little voice that follows me through life, whimpering, "You're getting better looking as you get older, but stay away from mirrors, old boy." After all, you can't have your egg and eat it too.

The Joyous Santa Parade

◦○◦○◦

About thirteen years ago, I took my grandsons, David and Michael, to a Santa Claus parade, and it got me to thinking.

Is it really a good thing to have the Santa Claus parade each year in winter? Couldn't there be a bill passed in the Commons to hold the Christmas parade in July when the weather would be more suitable? Who suffers from the cold, snowy wait for Kris Kringle more but the poor, frozen mothers, fathers and grandfathers, and who, by the end of the parade are wondering if there is a Lord, let alone a Santa.

And each winter, the parade is announced over and over on the radio, weeks in advance – always followed by an advertisement about what the stores have for good little kiddies. television and newspapers get kids cranked up to their highest pitch, inviting them to come see the motorless car that can almost talk and pick mushrooms, and Burping Baby Bertha who can spit up in three different shades just by gouging out one of her eyeballs. The ever-clanging Christmas carols then play on after each ad, tormenting mom and dad into promising little Joey that Santa will bring him an expensive car, even if they have to sell theirs at a loss.

But however I felt about it, I knew I couldn't be late for the parade, because if David and Michael lived to be ninety-seven, they'd never let me forget it. Since the parade began around 1:00 p.m., my advice to my daughter, Dianne, was to wake the boys up at 1:00 a.m. This still wouldn't have allowed enough time to get them ready, though Dianne and I

might have been ready by the time the parade started for
the men with the white uniforms and the net.

That morning we did as little talking as possible about
the parade. We talked about everything else, Trudeau, the
Red Brigades, and even the outlandish price of earth worms.
To silence all advertising, we plucked tubes from radio and
television. We then told the boys how we read that everyone,
young and old, human and inhuman, spacemen and astronauts, poor and rich alike, and even Michael Jackson, should
rest for an hour before a parade. It would make the time go
faster (and help the blood flow easier). Then we related a
ghastly story of how their great-grandparents had waited
for a parade one time. Their kids had got on their nerves so
badly, they slipped to the ground in a helpless heap, and
had to be carried off to an institution before Santa even
arrived (their blood not flowing at all).

We were careful not to give any liquids to the boys,
just bulk food – like dulse, cardboard boxes, sponge blot-
ters and the like. In fact, we hid all liquids, including Murine
for the eyes, sprays in bottles, anything that might remind
them they needed a drink. Instead, we showed them pictures of polar bears struggling to keep warm and Eskimoes
building huts in the frozen Arctic – pictures that were the
fathers of dryness, and would not create thirst. If there had
been a service station close by the parade route, we could
have phoned to ask them if they dehydrated children. As it
was, we reminded David and Michael about the bathroom
every half hour before the parade.

Amongst the crowd of people thronging both sides of
the street, we took our place behind an extremely tall man
who was wearing a wide-brimmed sombrero (and we weren't
even in Mexico). It cut off Michael's view completely. With
over two and a half hours for him to study the frame of the
man's overcoat, I was almost tormented to death with: "I

can't see a thing. Push him out of the way, Grampie." It was
a sin to teach Michael to be rude, so instead I suggested he
go up to this big man and say, "You might be a non-believer
in Santa, but move over some, and let me see the old chap."
But the tall man wouldn't budge an inch. (He was probably
waiting for a candy thrown by Santa.)

Now, David is not quite as shy as Michael. He had a
frog's eye view from between the tall man's legs. I prayed
the man wouldn't come to sudden attention, or I would have
witnessed the guillotining of my grandson's head.

But now Michael was missing, though for the past
twenty minutes he'd been crawling over every vein and
pore on my body, at times walking up my legs and across
my shoulders, as he strained to see the parade. But now he
was nowhere to be seen. Walking sideways, spear-shaped, I
struggled with my frontage, thrusting through throngs of
expectant Santa worshippers hemming us in. I asked strangers if they'd seen Michael, but got drowned out by the strains
of "Jingle Bells." One stubborn onlooker seemed cemented
to the sidewalk. I wondered if he'd let me through if I bit his
leg.

Suddenly, between verses of "Santa Claus Is Coming
To Town," I heard a familiar cry. I squeezed my way toward
the sound. Someone had trampled Michael's fingers and
his woollen cap was missing. Two large strawberry ears
were ready to snap from the cold, and there was an icicle
peeking out from his nose. Michael was sobbing and showing me three bloody fingers. Where was that Christmas
spirit? and for that matter, where in the Bible does it say anything about a Santa Claus parade? Finally, after straining
my memory for every item in Dr. Spock's baby and child
care book on how to stop Michael from throwing a tantrum,
(short of throwing one myself on top of the kid) he was
finally soothed when a float went by with Rudolph the Red-

nosed Reindeer. Obviously they hadn't spotted Michael's ears or he'd be on the float.

Michael now had to use the bathroom. I was expecting this. He'd only gone twenty-five minutes before we left home. For future parades I'd make sure the kids were hooked up directly to the sewer system.

Finally, before I went completely berserk, the big truck carrying Santa approached. Michael looked up with red eyes. David was still crouched between the large stranger's legs. The man didn't even know he was there because he hadn't moved. He was frozen to the pavement. Everyone was crowding in, cutting Michael's view again. He started screaming hysterically. I bent down to pick him up. He seemed much heavier – must have been the frost. At this point I discovered I'd been born with my arms too short because, as I grabbed the screeching Michael and tried to hoist him onto my shoulders, Santa was passing by and I just didn't have enough strength to get him up. I felt like yanking him off my hip, firing him at Santa and saying, "Here, you hold him for a while." Once again I strained with every ounce of strength in my tired frame to heave him onto my shoulders, and joy of joys, I made it. Off balance, sightless, bruised behind Michael's flying feet, and deaf from his maniacal bellowing, I heard "Merry Christmas. Ho, Ho, Ho." Thank heavens, it was over!

Suddenly, to make matters worse, Santa threw a candy – one in a scrimmage of ten kids. There were at least seven concussions and one near fatal heart attack. Quickly, I dragged Michael off my neck, grasped David's sticky hand (being so close to the ground, he'd snitched Santa's candy from the tall man), and beat it for the car. Before putting the boys in and locking the car, I took a good close look at them to make sure they were my grandsons, because kids lost at parades like this can (before they are found) develop into full-grown bearded men with canes, hearing aids, and hair growing out of their ears.

To keep them away from the stores, I promised them everything, candy, money, the keys to the car, even my will. And to keep them amused all the way home, I told them ghost stories, with an aside here and there that they themselves might turn into ghosts if they didn't quit biting each other.

Once home, I filled them full of candy and pop, and threw myself on the bed. I'd been up since 1:00 a.m. Then, I just listened to see if I could hear Santa's sleigh bells jingle in the night over my poor old jangled nerves.

We Come from a Broken Home

◦〇◦〇◦

Often, I'll meet a friend in a department store, and what they are buying looks good. And if I need the same item, they don't have to do much coaxing. Once I hear how economical it is and how it's even been known to save marriages, I buy one too (because it's too expensive to get married again). Theirs will last for years without the least bit of trouble – and in some cases even give birth to more of the same items – while ours will not last, no matter how well we treat it. Last! Why, it usually doesn't work from the minute we bring it into the house. (It's more important that I get my receipt than my change, so I can return the item.) I don't think we're retarded, and I do try to abide by the instructions.

Now, our neighbours look so comfortable when we see the pleasure they are getting from their new stove, iron, kettle, table and chairs. But my wife always finds a way to find fault with our new gadgets. She tells me that with Ruth's stove, all you do is turn the knob and the burner is red hot in seconds. Turn the same knob on ours and what happens? The burner barely gets warm (and me waiting for my porridge). Our oven works better, so I usually bake my porridge.

Then it was nutcrackers. A few weeks ago, I came across a set of nutcrackers on sale. And what's ninety-eight cents when it costs over a hundred dollars to enamel a tooth broken from biting into a sadistic walnut. Once home, I nestled the little pinchers in among a bowl of frightened

157

nuts. After filling the woodbox and falling into a chair to relax, my eyes turned in the direction of the nuts. A sigh of contentment eased out of me as I viewed the new crackers. A hard nut was slapped between the jaws of the shiny metal instrument. "I'll show you, Mr. Nut," I whispered as I closed my hand and squeezed the breath out of the nut, showing no pity. Suddenly, there was a limp feeling as though my fingers had fallen off. One of the metal arms, the strongest part of the cracker, had just broken in two! The lucky uncracked nut rolled along the carpet, laughing in its shell, with a look on its oval face as if to say, "Put me back up with the rest of the untouchables. We are having a ball waiting for some nut like you to crack us."

My next lemon was an electric can opener. Everybody I knew had one. They were time saving, they said, and made things so effortless. Some people even bragged how they could saw wood with theirs. But ours suffered from some terminal illness from the day I bought it. No matter how tender the metal in any can (even if it was cutting through tinfoil) our opener drained the hydro system so badly that the lights would blink. It made a deafening screech of sheer agony, as if it was cutting through three metal plates. The dog howled. The cat screeched, and we all had to wear those industrial earplugs each time we opened a can of beans.

Recently, we got a new colour television The first day I took it home, we all sat around as one happy family watching it. The next night, getting ready to enjoy myself once again, every picture looked as if they were advertising barbed wire fences. I pressed one little knob. Presto. The fences cleared up, but why all of a sudden was all the acting being done out of doors? We watched it snowing on the screen for hours. Finally, I gave it a smack, and it whined and went to sleep. The next night, Rhoda kept complaining to me about the heads that appeared on the screen. She said they were too big. The first payment was still warm and Rhoda was looking at me as though it was my fault that the man's head on the screen was that big. I told her that all the actors probably had water on the brain.

We also got a new radio a while ago. It would wait until everyone was listening intently to some exciting event like Idi Amin getting shot, then clam right up. When it came on again, the announcer would be talking about something altogether different – a new breed of worms; or how, by crossing a cabbage with a turnip, you could get catnip. We were listening to the news the other day about a hold-up. We even thought we knew some of the guys. Just as the announcer was about to give out the names and descriptions, we had to put up with complete silence for minutes (and thought it must have been a silent repeat program for Remembrance Day in July). When the radio came back on again, Perry F. Rockwood was telling us about the day of judgment. The day of judgment might have been upon *us* after missing that newscast, because those same men could have walked in our driveway and we'd never have known if they were the guilty culprits or not – at least not until they'd killed us.

Then there was the time Rhoda wanted an oil stove (this was a different stove than the one I baked my porridge in). All you had to do, people told us, was light it, turn a knob and in seconds the oven would be up to 350 degrees – ideal for bread baking and much faster than souping up a wood stove. Our friends had one that not only cooked the best loaves you ever saw, but almost mixed the dough by hand.

Well, what a time we had just to get it installed. I thought we'd have to jack up the house and slide it in underneath. After pinchbarring a few door frames, wall panels, and greasing the stove, we slipped it into the kitchen. That stove was beautiful to look at and listen to during cold frosty days. But no matter how much heat was thrown from the *stove*, the *oven* stayed cool and quiet. I've seen Rhoda leave bread in there for four hours to find it still with that tubercular look. Of course it was my fault. Rhoda said I must have been drunk when I bought it. I guess I should have taken it out for a trial run, and cooked up a batch of lasagna in that oven right in the store.

Rhoda finally got tired of complaining and calling down the Company. And where it took three strong husky lads to set up the stove, it took only one skinny man to heave the whole trouble-making hunk of iron out into the yard.

Now, a few years back, we got a new floor furnace, with a nice, steady flow of oil piped in from a two-hundred-gallon tank. Praying for icy cold winds and frigid weather to try out the furnace, we didn't have long to wait. And it was lucky for us this stormy night that the howling winds shook us awake. The house was black with smoke. At the stage where we were supposed to be dead, I rushed downstairs to see what hymns they'd sing at our funeral, and found out that the oil plus some water particles had frozen on the way in from the outside. The furnace had gone out. Then, as the dribbling oil hit the hot pan, it just smoked furiously like Krakatoa – until I shut the oil off from the tank outside.

This still happens from time to time and that's why our daughter presented us with the best item we've ever had (and that's really lived up to its name): the smoke detector. About the time we got it, Rhoda and I had quit smoking so it wouldn't start coughing over our cigarette fumes. With an oil furnace and two wood stoves going full blast, the detector was a welcome guest. I was even thinking of claiming it as a dependent on my income tax.

We hung it by a nail on the ceiling, as per the instructions, and that was it – our guardian angel. We named it Burpey. After installing it, we felt so safe sleeping on the second floor that we wouldn't have objected if the government had decided to use our premises as an artillery range or a bomb drop. If they'd dropped the A-bomb on us, Burpey would have saved us. After all, wasn't our watchdog clinging to the ceiling like a bat at the bottom of the steps, just waiting for one puff of smoke to bark its batteries out and save its masters from asphyxiation? This one night at 2:00 a.m., choking black smoke nudged us awake. Old Burpey downstairs had slept right through it. We soon discovered that when the house was thick with smoke, Burpey was as happy as a lark (he might have given off inner beeps that couldn't be heard by the human ear). It was the cold air Burpey despised. On mild days, we would cut the oil off to the furnace, and the detector would torment us all day long with little short burps. God help us if we ever opened a window in zero weather. The lovely fresh air hurt its lungs so bad that it would make sickening belches every thirty seconds until we closed the window. It even made a good watchdog, because it would start burping as soon as a stranger came in the house.

We've had this place so full of smoke, you'd have thought Vesuvius was erupting and the smoke detector never even cleared its throat. I'm sure if a raging fire was in force, it would be filled with such happiness and contentment that it might even break into a snore. But I've watched it carefully at the times when it's supposed to beep, and it acts sort of embarrassed, as if it knows it should, but just can't get the words out.

In the meantime, we now have a block and tackle set above our bed. And when we are awakened by the smell of smoke in our nostrils, we each put an arm through a sling as I pull down on the feeder rope. Then we lower ourselves out through the window and onto the frozen ground below. Because of the cold, we're always prepared, and like Laplanders we wear terribly heavy clothing to bed, like ski suits, coveralls, and woollen hip boots.

The smoke that occasionally fills the house may also have affected the fridge. If it isn't the smoke, we'll have to call in a psychic healer, because it squeaks and snorts all day long, and at times lets go with a cry just like a baby. But it is something we can live with, and it's good company when you're home alone. You feel like you're baby sitting a baby pig.

Now, we have three toilets. The third one is an outhouse. That's the one I generally use; the outside one, the one you can trust. It's so much safer. I don't have to worry about the bowl overflowing while I'm half dressed and looking for higher ground – as the water pours down through the ceiling into the kitchen. The outhouse is my favourite winter or summer and, in the spring, you can listen to the robins singing as they have a nest right outside the door.

But with the toilets in the house, either the float is stuck, the handle is broken, the power is off, the pump's kaput, or there's something clogged. I've been dealing with this for years. So I tell Rhoda, "There's two holes on the one outside. Why don't you bring a lunch and come out and explain to me the troubles you're having in the house."

If you don't think we have all these troubles, why not come spend the day with us – if you dare. And if you know a good exorcist, bring him along too. We could use him. Also, be sure to bring your own nutcrackers, a can opener, ear plugs, a gas mask, something that will provide you with warmth (like five layers of reindeer skins), a pot, and lots of old rags (that's old rags, not old bags; although you could bring the latter too). They'd be a great help in cleaning up the kitchen after the toilet has overflowed its banks. And if you have a smoke detector, bring it to our place and have it tested.

As I write this, I just got an important call to be fifty miles from here on business. I rush out to my little truck. The front tire is flat and frozen in the ice. My spare is up-town in the garage. My wife is over at her sister's. My hens just broke out of their coop and my water pump won't stop running. . . .